GOING TO WORK ON A YAK

Giles Holtom's memoirs

Mark Holtom

ISBN-13: 9798757145440

Cover design by: Art Painter
Library of Congress Control Number: 2018675309
Printed in the United States of America

CONTENTS

Title Page

Copyright

Part 1: Going to work on a Yak   1

1.   It's as true as I'm sitting here on this bike   2

2.   Oh, to be a Farmer's Boy.   7

3.   You're in the Army now.   24

4.   The Veterinary Corps   27

5.   You're going on a little holiday.   36

6.   A Soldier goes to war.   46

7.   Men in Grey Coats   54

8.   Court Martial at Wadi Yerwanna   59

9.   Lion around in Addis   66

10.   Crete   71

11.   Egypt   76

12.   Germany   97

13.   The road to Singapore   116

14.   The road to Hong Kong   138

15.   And so, in conclusion   153

PART II: Decline, Fall and Rise.   158

16.   What happened Next?   159

17.   Beside the seaside, beside the sea (A new life)   171

18.   We'll keep a welcome in the hillside.   194

19.   Final curtain   211

Part III: It's not me. It's my family.   215

20.   Larry the Lamb   216

21.   The 13th Hole.   220

22.   A Holtom Death   228

PART 1: GOING TO WORK ON A YAK

1.   IT'S AS TRUE AS I'M SITTING HERE ON THIS BIKE

This book is a history of my father, Giles Holtom's life. It is told in an oral style, much the same way as Giles told me these stories, from when my brothers and I were children, sitting at the dinner table.

The stories were wild, imaginative and exciting. I believed them because, well, I was 7 at the time, and he was my dad. It was only in later life, when I retold the stories to other people, that I realised their inherent lack of believability.

"Tell us about the baby elephant," I would demand. "No, the one about the emperor's lion," countered my brother. Usually Giles would tell us about something totally different, that had just occurred to him. "Did I tell you about when I was arrested as a spy?" he would start.

Some stories became more adult, as I was older and he retold them to me. The gist was the same, just some of the details got filled in.

In the last year of his life, I brought Giles to visit my new house in Suffolk for a short holiday. During the days, we would drive over to Essex to the villages where he had lived and worked as a lad. As we drove, he would tell me some more stories as a place would trigger a memory. In the evenings, we sat and drank and talked. I wanted him to retell all of his stories, realising that he would never have the time or energy to write them all down. We spent many hours together, reviewing and discussing his stories, but this time I tried to remember them so they could be documented.

Some new stories came out that I had never heard before. Some details and new characters were revealed that had remained secret for over 60 years. With this book, some of them can finally come to light.

Lastly, he told me some more recent stories that included me, and I learned a little about my life and its context with my father and mother.

I decided to put them down on paper, and to do so, I tried to get access to his Army records, so I could put the stories into some form of chronological sequence. Whatever the reason, the Army were unable to provide this information. Maybe it was because of his involvement with people he called 'men in grey coats' - meaning military intelligence, or maybe it was something to do with the fact that one person, throughout his army career, was actively trying to get him killed, or at least badly hurt. It is almost as if they had been redacted. You might find the reason for this in the stories, as they unfold.

There were just so many questions. How is it that he spoke fluent Arabic? What ever happened to the baby elephant he got me? Why did so many strange, uninvited people turn up at his funeral, including representatives from Princess Anne and Prince Charles?

So it was down to me to investigate the details of his life and set a sequence and timeline to the stories and the places he visited. I researched the background history of what was happening in a country when Giles was there. I was amazed at what I found.

Amongst other places, he was in Austria when it was partitioned, Egypt during the fight for independence, and Malaya and Burma during the communist uprisings.

He was behind the iron curtain at least twice, arrested as a spy (by the Americans), court martialled and awarded a medal from the same action, court martialled (again) and then promoted (again).

He visited 46 countries, before British Airways existed and could take you there. Mostly he got there by walking or hitching, on trains, boats and lorries. Sometimes he rode there on camels, donkeys or yaks.

Finally, to help you visualise Giles as you read his stories, I would ask you to picture someone walking like a country boy with his feet at 10 to 2 like Charlie Chaplin. This was the way Giles ambled though his life. Not too fast. Not too slow.

So now you know a little about Giles, on with the book.

Not all of this is true. If you pressed me, I would guess that about 90% is true, and the other 90% is made up.

The people and situations are real. I have spoken with the army comrades that are still alive, and they read the draft of the book. They confirm that all of the stories are true, albeit embroidered and characterised (by me) rather than bluntly stated as they would be in army reports.

The majority of names used have been made up, mostly because I couldn't be bothered to remember them and sometimes to protect the guilty who were real bastards. You will learn who they are.

Holtom is quite a rare family name. The Holtom surname is the $217,512^{th}$ most common last name on a global scale, borne by approximately 1 in 3,866,072 people.

And yet, we get everywhere.

There were probably Holtom's on the beach at Hastings in 1066, helping the Normans park their boats.

"That'll be two pennies for the day, or a groat and I'll make sure that no-one nicks your oars."

But family names, until after the Elizabethan period, had many variants in spelling, and there are many from the same family named Holtom whose brother was named Holton or Haulton.

The best example I could find was William Haulton from Holton St Mary in Suffolk who at 23, sailed to Massachusetts on the Francis in 1634. In the first census he is named William Holtom and yet both his sons were named Holton.

Closer to home, there are several branches of Holtom's in the UK, most notably in and around Stratford on Avon Warwickshire.

In fact, I'll tell you a 'true' family story.

Now, you should know that Holtom's have always been good natterers and prone to tell a story at the drop of a hat. And it is a well-known family secret that Shakespeare got all of his best ideas from Joseph Holtom, mostly in the White Swan Stratford, over a pint.

You see Joseph Holtom could tell a story, but William Shakespeare could write.

"Hey Joe, tell me that one about the Prince of Denmark again," said Shakespeare readying his quill.

"What, 'amlet? OK. Mine's a pint"

If you don't believe me, go to Holy Trinity Church in Stratford, where William Shakespeare is buried, go outside between the nave and the river, and you will see several old gravestones set into the ground, walked on by tourists as they stroll by, looking for a patch of grass to sit and eat their sandwiches.

A closer inspection will show you that they are Holtom's, buried on and around 1615, and as such direct contemporaries of the bard himself.

Not only this, but walk away from the church along college lane and the 2nd street on the left is Holtom Street.

And there, down in Essex, there is another Branch of Holtom's, and this is where Giles was born in 1931.

2. OH, TO BE A FARMER'S BOY.

All of Giles' early life was published in another book, "A funny little old boy" and won't be covered here.

Giles' dad Ernest William Holtom (Bill) was a cow man on a farm near East Hanningfield, Essex. Just before the war he and the family all moved up around Halstead which is a middling small town of 27,000 people.

The war affected many things at home as well as at the front, and in Giles' case, his mother, Hilda, ran off with a soldier. As Bill was in the RAF, as a gunner flying Wellingtons, there was no-one to look after Giles and he was shuffled around from grandparent to aunt to uncle throughout the war. He was a cross between being part of the family and an unwanted suitcase.

His grandparents had a large house in Halstead and they had several land girls billeted with them for the duration. Land girls were young women that worked the land in place of the farm labourers who had all been conscripted.

In 1947, Bill was finally demobbed, and at the same time Giles, who was 16, had also moved back home. One girl, Joan, was still staying there and working on the land and despite a gap of nearly 20 years in ages, Bill got very friendly with Joan, in fact ousting another suitor and claiming her for his own.

Two things happened around this time; the first started with a

Sunday lunch.

The family all sat down, as usual, for a Sunday lunch. Just about the time for passing the carrots, grandma Pauline announced that, if they weren't doing anything next Saturday, they were all invited to the church to see her and grandad get married.

"Married!" blustered uncle Derek, "but you've been married since 1914, haven't you?"

"Just a minute," said Bill, "if you're not married, that means that I'm a basta.."

"You all are," interrupted gran.

And so the story had to be told.

Grandad was one of two brothers. Being French they were called Jean and Jacques. They were Huguenots, who are basically French protestants, that had sought refuge in the UK.

Jacques Pauline, the elder by 2 years, was married to Amelie (grandma). And all three lived together happily, in the east end of London.

In 1914, in a spate of patriotic fervour, Jacques announced that he was going to enlist with the French army to kill the Boche. He was killed at Verdun.

Jean Pauline, with no less fervour, but slightly more brains, joined the British army. He suggested to the enlisting sergeant that, as he was fluent in French, he would be most valuable at the rear translating for the generals. The army in their wisdom posted Jean to India, gave him a rifle and told him to guard a well.

He came back to London in 1919, with a dim view of the British army and a passable ability to swear in Hindi.

Back in London, Jean went back to stay with his brother's widow, and being French, neither thought too much about getting together, and so they did. After all, they already had a marriage certificate in their surname, and both their names matched on their passports. The only problem was that the locals in the street, also knew, and this was not the done thing, so they packed their bags and moved, away from prying eyes, out of London to Essex.

In 1949, the British government amended a law which prevented a man marrying his brother's widow, and on hearing this, grandma and grandad Pauline decided to get married. Bastards and all.

The second thing that happened, was that Bill decided that he didn't want to go back to working as a farm labourer and there wasn't enough room, even in the big old house, for all to live comfortably, so Bill went off, found and rented a cheap cottage in Gainsford End about 7 miles away.

Gainsford End is a hamlet near Toppesfield, Essex. It consisted of about 15 houses, no church but it did have a pub.

Giles' family lived opposite the pub in a half thatched, half tin-roofed cottage. His first job of the day was to get up at 5am to light the primus stove and have it hot and working, so that Joan, his new step-mother (who was only about 5 years older than him) could come down and start cooking the breakfast

Having decided that he wasn't going to spend the rest of his life looking at cow's arses, Bill had hit upon the idea of the motor trade. After the war every single car made by the British was sent abroad, to help pay off the country's war debts and loans. It was impossible to buy a new Morris or Austin. Given that all new cars went abroad, there was a massive unfulfilled need in the marketplace, and Bill was just the kind of guy to fill it.

He knew of several old cars holed up in the backs of barns, and set about liberating them, and making a profit in the process. Most cars responded, with a little bit of coaxing and occasional brute force, and in the end, he was able to push an assortment of mostly running cars out onto a happy and uncritical populace.

One of the problems of living in such a small village was that the community was tiny, consisting of around 50 people. And everybody knew everybody else. More importantly, there was no such thing as a secret. If you farted outside your front door, people would know about it by the time you got to the end of the street.

"Mike tells me that you just farted outside your house." Yes. This was country living.

So, being 16, finding a girlfriend was basically a selection of 2 girls, both of whom Giles had known and who knew him. It was time to get on his bicycle to see what other villages offered.

Giles was a naturally chatty and affable person, but he was instantly tongue tied when faced with a girl of his own age. He longed to be able to chat to girls effortlessly like his mate Dougie Drane. They would go out to parties and dances and within 5 minutes, Dougie, having spotted a couple of girls, selected the pretty one and separated her from her friend, had a girl on his arm.

"Her mate over there wants a drink," Dougie would say as he steered his new conquest around the back of the scout hut to see how far she would let him go.

Giles would approach the sullen mate, get her a drink, in recompense for which she would scowl at him and stalk off looking for more interesting boys.

It was at one church summer party, when the afternoon fete had changed into an evening dance, that Giles' luck changed.

As usual Dougie had already paired off and was smooching with a girl on the dance floor, and as usual, Giles was strategically placed by the drinks table, hoping that a girl would talk to him when she came to pick up a squash. He was stunned into bumbling silence when this ploy actually worked.

"Hello Giles. Do you like American music?" said Veronica Witty as she sat by the side of him. She was a girl from Toppesfield who was not only beautiful, but known to 'give out'.

"arfnglk," said Giles. He swallowed, "Fnghkui," He tried again.

"Do you smoke? I am gasping for a fag," said Veronica, taking control of the situation.

Giles fumbled a packet of Woodbines out of his pocket, and held them, upside down, for her inspection.

"I like Passing Clouds," She said. "Never mind. Come on." And taking him by the hand, walked outside.

She walked him to the far side of the graveyard, and into the shade, under the boughs of a willow.

"No-one can see us here," said Veronica. "I hate being watched. Don't you?"

"Urp."

"Where is that fag?"

He took out two cigarettes and placed them both in his mouth and lit them. He had seen some American guy do this in a film. Maybe he couldn't speak but he would show her he was cool.

His lips were dry and taking one cigarette out of his mouth, he peeled a layer of the skin off his lip. With a yip, he handed the cigarette to Veronica, with a slice of his skin attached. The end of the cigarette had a drop of blood on it. She didn't seem to notice.

In fact she only took two puffs from the cigarette before throwing it on the ground.

"I've been watching you."

"erm."

"In fact, I was wondering what you thought of these?" she said, unbuttoning her blouse. "Would you like to touch them?"

"Fnargh," thought Giles, but he managed not to say it. Instead he reached forward to grasp the proffered breast with a trembling hand.

It crunched.

He recoiled. He was sure they weren't supposed to do that. "Oh my God, I've broken it," he thought.

"Sor.. Sor.., er."

"It's OK. That's just the padding," she said pulling out some tissue and throwing it over her shoulder. "Now try."

Giles realised that it wasn't very romantic holding one breast in his hand at arm's length, and so, moved in to kiss her. Tssssss went her hair on his cigarette.

"Oh, for fuck's sake, come here," said Veronica, throwing away his cigarette and pulling him toward her.

"Take your pants off," she said, whilst expertly removing her knickers and laying on top of a gravestone.

"oh."

Back in the party, Giles wanted to show Veronica off to Dougie.

"Wait here" he said, but when he had found his friend and returned, she had disappeared.

"She's gone home," said one of her friends, "You've got blood on your lip."

Two weeks later, the news around the village was that Veronica Witty was going to marry Bill Mellis and that it was going to be done quickly. They were even rushing the banns.

The rumour was that she had got knocked up by Brian Teal, but that he wouldn't marry her, so she went out and found some guy as a patsy, shagged him once, and then persuaded him to marry her as he had 'made her pregnant' on their first try. Her dad was most insistent. Apparently, the baby was born 7 months after they were married. If you go to Halstead today, you can still see him, all grown up, and looking for all the world like Brian Teal.

This was a common occurrence in and around the villages in Essex at this time.

It gave rise to the joke about a young man who tells his dad that he wants to marry the girl at the dairy to which the dad replies that this would not be possible.

"Why," asked the boy.

"Because, 20 years ago, I was a bit friendly with her mother, and truth be told, she might be your sister."

The son runs, sobbing indoors and meets his mother, who asks why he is so sad. The son tells his mum, to which she replies, "You can marry her if you want. He isn't your real father."

So, it seems that Giles being an inept lover had caused him to dodge a bullet. Never mind, there would be other opportunities, both to be inept and to be a lover.

In the last year of the war and just after, at the age of 15 or so,

Giles had signed up as a farrier's apprentice. rather than work for his dad for free. It helped bring money into the house, and left a little for him to spend on himself.

The apprenticeship was actually a very defined process, regulated by the London Guild called the Worshipful Company of Farriers. It lasted 7 years (!) and for the most part was basically legal servitude. It, like farriery itself, was a hangover from mediaeval times, and the rules and formats had been laid out for hundreds of years.

Most 15-year-old apprentices were good for nothing more than fetching coke and working the bellows. It turned out that Giles was a quick, apt and able learner. Apparently as well as being academically capable, he was good with his hands and easily grasped the skills necessary for this trade.

This meant that the smith could use Giles to do more exact and demanding work, which in turn meant he could earn more money.

In those days, everything was made by hand from iron stock, not just the shoes, and Giles spent many hours heating and pounding iron bars to make bags of horseshoe nails, clout nails, gate hinges and door latches.

By 16 he was a well grown boy, and capable of shoeing even the largest of horses, and he enjoyed it. Often being called by the farrier to go and do some work whilst he was out on a stable visit, away from the forge.

Giles still had another 5 years of his apprenticeship to do, but the writing was on the wall. Even in the wilds of Essex, the internal combustion engine was replacing the horse, and there was more need for a garage mechanic than there was for a farrier. But he wasn't bothered, as he had no intention of finishing this apprenticeship and he wasn't going to be a farrier, a blacksmith or a farm hand. No. His mind was set on bigger and better things.

I thought I would add a village story in Giles' own words, from his files.

"I have known people in my youth who have only ever left the village for the local town, and that no more than a couple of times a year. One man I knew that lived in Gainsford End, when we lived there, went by train to London, as a special treat. This he did from Yeldham Station all of 3 miles from Gainsford End, with a change of train at Marks tey. It was promoted as a special day trip at a cheap rate, and he took it. As I said, it was only for the day, and as he walked home that night he called in the village pub for a pint, and to tell us all about his exciting trip. Everyone from the village must have gone at various times in the evening to hear his story. I did. I was told by my father to go and hear it. The main thing that he was excited about was that you didn't get wet in London, as it was covered over in glass, just like a ginormous green house.

I thought it hilarious because of what I thought of as my sophistication and superior knowledge, realising that he had not even left Liverpool Street Station. Of course he had been misled because the Station itself was bigger than our village and had a lot more shops and attractions inside it than there were within the next 10 miles of our village. Looking back, no wonder he was taken in. I think it took the army to change all that for me."

◆ ◆ ◆

Making money was an important part of life, and if Giles wanted anything, he had to earn it himself. He would often get a couple of shillings from a shoeing, or for fixing or making something in the forge. But by far his biggest money earner was his Jack Russel terrier, Charlie.

Charlie was a prize ratter, and he and Giles would walk all around the farms, over the fields and through the barns in search of rats. Charlie would pounce and throw the rats up into the air, trying to break their backs. Those that ran away, Giles would dispatch with his .410.

Charlie and Giles were a lethal combination. More importantly, they were a profitable combination. Rats were a scourge and ate the crops, and each rat tail, presented to the village policeman, would get a government bounty payment of 6d.

After a good Saturday afternoon's work, Giles was often able to pocket 5 shillings for 10 tails. But this was not all, as the policeman never took the rats tails (why would he?), so Giles would walk up to the farm and present the same tails to the farmer for another 5 shillings.

After a summer's worth of ratting, Giles had enough money to buy an old motorbike.

Bill had bought two motorbikes for £6. One was a Matchless 350, running and in good order, and the other was a couple of boxes of bits which purported to be a Red panther 250. Bill sold the panther to Giles for £6! He wasn't one to miss the opportunity to make a profit, even off his own son.

The career's advice in Giles' school was straightforward. If you got A's then go to university, B's and C's become an accountant, and the rest were advised to either join the army or work on the land.

For Giles this presented a problem as on the one hand his life as an unpaid car mechanic for his dad was predetermined but academically, he was a sharp minded and bright student. He had excelled in Maths and technical drawing, and at 16 he was good enough to be awarded a bursary and scholarship to help pay to continue his education, take his A levels and then to go and study to be an architect. Fuck farming. This was his desire. His plan. His next step.

He was excited to be able to go home and announce that he could go to college, and the family didn't have to pay. This was important. Even more importantly, it meant that he wouldn't spend the rest of his life working on a farm, in a garage or propping up the corner of a horse's arse.

Unfortunately, these arguments didn't make a difference to his father. The family needed money and there would be no possibility for him to go onto further education. He had to keep earning, either by working for free for his dad or by getting a job and bringing money into the house.

His plans and hopes were dashed and in pieces.

So he had no choice but to leave school at 16, but in a fit of teenage pique, he refused to work for his father and went out looking for a job. Within a week, he had signed up to do bomb disposal. After all, the money was good.

The war had been over for a couple of years now, but there were still hundreds of tons of bombs dotted around Essex and the South East In general.

It was the common tactic to keep munitions and fuel away from aerodromes. That way, if they were attacked, the enemy would not destroy everything, and the bombing flights could begin again as soon as new munitions were brought in from the caches and any runway damage had been repaired.

Of course, the bombs and fuel were kept reasonably nearby, so they could be collected and used when needed. But where? The answer was hidden in plain sight, in some of the little copses, glades and spinneys dotted in the fields around the area. After all, who would bomb a field? Many fields had little stands of trees. How were the Germans to know which ones contained piles of munitions?

As for the bombs themselves, they continued to be made, right up until the last day of the war, so there were huge stockpiles of them littered around the landscape, and it was Giles' new job to drive to each of these secret caches and defuse the bombs hidden there.

For Giles, this was a great job. It was easy, highly paid and gave him the money to buy his AJS 350, on which he spent a large part of him time, driving from cache to cache.

It was also pretty safe. After all, these were new, fresh bombs, not ones that had been thrown out of a plane. All he really needed to do was unscrew the detonator off the nose and the remainder was inert. They newly defused bombs were simply picked up, put into trucks and taken to Harwich, where they were loaded onto ships that dumped them out somewhere in the North Sea.

Bombs come in all shapes and sizes, and Giles' favourite was incendiaries. They were small and relatively light and easy to handle, but by far the most important thing was that each came with its own silk parachute, which he could liberate and sell in the local pub. They were considered perks of the job.

Armed with his supply of silk, he could venture into town on a Saturday night where he could sell it to women who wanted the silk to make their own underwear instead of the rationed, coarse, utilitarian products sold in the shops.

Quite often he never made it to the pub and would be ambushed as soon as he drove into town on his bike.

"Are you the guy with the silk?"

"Yes."

"How much?"

"5/-."

It should be said that 5/- (5 shillings) was enough to buy 5 or 6 pints of beer, which was a good night out.

Of course, not all women could afford or wanted to pay him for the silk, and offered alternative payment methods, like a glimpse of the finished article next week. Strangely enough, given his previous ineptitude with women, he wasn't averse to these alternatives, and gladly tried to help the women out when he could.

Funnily enough, in these transactions, he often got to see the handiwork, in some cases, even to see and enjoy the delights that were underneath, but even though this happened several times, afterwards the women simply went back to their own lives, and in some cases, their own boyfriends and even husbands, without a backward glance. There was never a "shall I see you again," or "do you want to take me to the pictures." So he was having sex, but didn't have the responsibility of having a girlfriend with it.

Yes. He was now 17 and Bomb disposal was a great job.

Within 6 months, Giles had saved up enough money to upgrade to a Velocette 500.

This was the newest and fastest bike he had ever owned, and he set off to Halstead to show off his new acquisition to his mates. He parked up on the pavement outside the Bull on the high street and waited to be noticed.

"Hey, Giles. Is that yours?"

"What does it go like?"

"Had a ton out of it on the Braintree road," said Giles nonchalantly.

The 'Velo' was black and gold and famous for having a stylish fish tail exhaust, and being a teenager, he had removed most of the baffles from the silencer to make it louder (and therefore sound faster).

"What does it sound like?"

"Listen to this," he said, as he kicked it over and revved it.

The sound reverberated up and down the street, drawing envious looks from his friends. And it was with a showman-like blip of the throttle, he reached over to pull in the decompressor and stop the engine, when it backfired spectacularly.

The whole fishtail end of the silencer exploded off the back of the exhaust and shot through the plate glass window of the pub.

Time to leave.

It was no big deal being banned from a pub in Halstead. There were 27 pubs for a population of 27,000 people. It was the most pubbed town in Britain. There were still another 26 left to go drinking in.

When he was 18, Giles received a cunningly worded invitation from the British Government to join the Army. He had to go. It was 1948 and Britain had National Service, which was 18 months in the Army for £2.10s a week.

All males aged 18 had to register for National Service, another name for "you are going in the army, air force or navy" and no excuses taken, except for illness or something like a missing leg or arm.

So four times a year, boys between the ages of 17 and 9 months and 18, had to go to the local labour exchange and register with all their details. If you didn't go, then the police came and did it for you. This was very nice of them, though while they were about it, they put you in prison for a couple of weeks, so they knew where to find you when it was time to go.

During the next three months, they were called to a medical centre to see if they could find the arm or leg that you said you hadn't got.

I must say they were pretty good at it; they found Charlie Combs and his father (that he said had died). That is why Colin said he needed exemption, to support his poor old mother etc. So you see some good came out of it. They had a hell of a party when they found the father in the shed at the bottom of the garden.

At the enrolment, Giles was interviewed to see what the best options would be for him, and which part of the army he would join.

"Any skills?" asked a Sergeant.

"I'm just a farm boy," replied Giles.

"Hmmm. Infantry then."

"I'm also an apprentice Farrier."

"You don't say. Hang on a minute." The sergeant riffled through some papers, eventually pulling one out and spreading it onto the desk.

"They're looking for one of those, here."

"Who?"

"The 'ousehold Cavalry. 'Bunch of posh boys wiv 'orses."

"I could do that."

"No, you can't sunshine. This is for regular army, not fuckin' national service.
Of course, you could be just right for the job, but you'd 'ave to join the regulars."

"How long?"

"5 years. But you get £4 a week."

It took about 10 seconds for Giles to realise that not only would he be in a posh part of the army in Westminster, far away from any farm, but he would be earning more than double for doing it. On top of that, he probably wouldn't have to carry a rifle and march everywhere.

"Where do I sign?"

He was going to be a farrier after all.

Meanwhile in the news:

Halstead Gazette
Veronica Witty to marry Bill Mellis. Police searching motorcyclist who broke pub window. Inspector looking into silk knickers.

Daily Telegraph
Government updates Marriage Law, allowing Widows remarriage to Brother-in-Law

3.   YOU'RE IN THE ARMY NOW.

Basic training was at a camp in Warwickshire. No matter what regiment you were going to eventually, you first had to become a soldier. So, Giles with about 50 other teenagers, was subjected to all of the normal hardships of basic training.

Let's face it for the majority of them, this was the first time they had ever eaten three meals a day. Not only that, they were young and unburstable. Yes, running 5 miles in army boots was a pain, but 10 minutes after they got back, had a brew and a fag, they were ready to go again.

So for 6 weeks they went running, climbing hills, and marching. Then back to barracks for cleaning rifles, boots and belt buckles, and they all loved it.

At the end of basic, Giles was given his new orders.

"There is no travel pass for me to get to London," said Giles.

"You don't need one where you're going."

"Where's that?" asked Giles.

"Right here, Private Holtom. You're in the Warwickshire Fusiliers."

"There must be some mistake. I'm not in the infantry. I'm supposed to be with the Household Cavalry."

"The army doesn't make mistakes, Holtom. Now, get fell in."

And that was that – almost.

About 10 days after his posting, he was called to see to Commanding Officer.

"It seems that the army has made a mistake," he said, "We've just received your paperwork saying you should be with the Household Cavalry."

"Thank you, sir."

"There is a small problem. Apparently, the Cavalry got tired of waiting for you and have filled the position. So you can't go there, and the army says you don't belong here. Do you have any preferences?"

"Where can I go, sir?"

"Well, there is the Veterinary Corps, just down the road in Melton Mowbray. They have horses. I'll give them a call if you want."

And so it was, that Giles became Private Holtom in the Royal Army Veterinary Corps.

Meanwhile in the news:

Halstead Gazette
Veronica Mellis (nee Witty) has baby boy. Mother doing well. "We understand that the baby was slightly premature, but he is surprisingly strong and healthy," says doctor.

4. THE VETERINARY CORPS

T he Royal Army Veterinary Corps is responsible for looking after and maintaining the field army's animals. Initially, this meant horses up to and including WW1, but as warfare changed, the use of horses became much less common, and by the end of WW2, they concentrated on mules (as pack animals in difficult terrain) and dogs.

The Royal Army Veterinary Corps is one of the smallest Regiments in the British Army. It is also one of the strangest in this (or any) army. It consisted of never more than 150 men, when fully up to strength, and was spread throughout the whole of the world in small detachments.

The RAVC had the distinction of having a uniform that was first issued in 1901 and had not changed since then. This was probably because they had a lot left over from the First World War, and were not going to throw them away. Giles' uniform was stamped "1914" on the inside.

The army organises itself into consistent groups, like infantry, engineers, artillery, etc., and as a general rule, soldiers travel in groups together; regiments, battalions, or even platoons.

The veterinary corps is different. They look after the army's animals, such as horses, mules and dogs. Now, as these animals are all spread throughout the rest of the army, each regiment or battalion may require a vet to look after their particular animals, but given the number of animals, they only need one or possible two vets, per regiment. Thus the veterinary corps is spread throughout the rest of the army, rather than as one single, homogeneous group.

This in turn leads to quite different behaviour from their soldiers. They are to one side, and not part of the normal rank and file, and as such, are often just as happy mixing with officers, NCOs as well as privates.

It was perfectly normal for a vet to be chatting with a brigadier about the welfare of his horse, as much as he was chatting with a private about his guard dog. Vets were often invited guests into the officer's, and sergeant's messes, rather than just mixing with the other ranks.

The other thing that stood out, was the fact that they were famously independent characters. Whilst every other soldier had to conform with a routine set down by the army (and his sergeant), the vets had a lot more leeway in their activities. They didn't have to go on route marches, or do square bashing, and in general, they didn't stand guard duty or perform such menial chores that were the norm for most soldiers.

This doesn't mean that they never did these things, but for the most part, they were 'exempt'.

So, as a general rule, each group of 'normal' soldiers might have one or possibly two vets. The main exception was Germany.

This was 1950, and Germany was occupied by large contingents of both British and American forces. In turn there were lots of allied bases. They had come after WW2 but had stayed on as part of NATO, in confrontation with Russia and her allies, just over the border in East Germany.

Given that there were British Army groups dotted throughout the landscape, it made sense to have the veterinary corps as a group, in one central place, which could be deployed to any other

Regiment as required. In the RAVC's case, this place was Paderborn in Westphalia – but more of that later.

The final part of being weird (independent) was that the vets often had to travel from A to B on their own.

If the army wanted a platoon, or more, soldiers to go to a place, then the logistics would be put into play. Trucks, supplies, support were all set up, so that the group could be moved efficiently to wherever they were needed.

The army's logistics didn't extend down to individuals, and it was common practice for a vet to be given orders to present himself at a certain place, and an army travel chit.

Travel chits are unusual bits of paper. Where possible, they include details of transport available, but in some cases, they are a form that says something like,

> *"His Majesty's Government requests and requires that*
> *you provide every assistance to the bearer in travelling*
> *to his nominated destination.*
>
> *Any costs incurred by you in performance of this duty, can be presented as an invoice to your nearest British Consulate for payment."*

In this case, it basically says, get there whatever way you can. The initiative required to fulfil this bred a certain kind of independence of thought and action and this was common amongst the vets.

What about expenses? Well the soldier would probably have some cash on him, but this was mostly British pounds which were not much use in the desert. The Army certainly wasn't Thomas Cook and they didn't issue travellers cheques to the soldiers, nor indeed did they provide body belts with sovereigns stitched into the hem. This means that the soldier would also have to use the chitty and his own scrounging skills if he wanted to eat on the trip.

◆ ◆ ◆

It is worth mentioning a couple of people that Giles would meet in the corps; Sandy and CSM (Company Sergeant Major) Crisp.

Sandy was sone of the first people Giles met at Melton.

"Y'all roight then, ba?" asked Sandy in his 'sloight' Suffolk accent.

"Foine, Booiee," replied Giles with his neighbouring Essex twang.

"What's yor noime?"

"Goyles," he answered.

"Jolly. Good enough," said Sandy and Jolly was born.

"Howd that dawg, Jol." It was one of Sandy's schoolmates, Podge Holder, that had asked the teacher, "is there a 'W' in dawg, 'cos that's the way it sounds."

So, if nothing else, at least there was someone he could talk to and understand.

It was hard to judge Sandy's age. He was definitely old, but you couldn't really tell how old. Sandy was a Sergeant and the rumour was that he had been in the corps since before the war.

In any case, he was big. Not really tall, but certainly wide, with hands like dinner plates.

It turned out that Sandy had previously been a fairground boxer. The type that young hopefuls would try to last three one-minute rounds with for £5. This would always play out the same way. A Barker would call out to the virility and vanity of some of the farm or factory boys that had come to the fair.

Sandy would let the first one get in a few good shots, and almost win, and then all of his mates would have to have a go, to prove their manliness. Anyway £5 was a lot of money.

Surprisingly, he wasn't a vicious man and he would happily parry and swat blows away and not get angry as the young men grew more and more agitated, trying to land a punch. Then, Sandy would seemingly tap them once lightly on the chin. His punches weren't the massive, haymaker blows, that we see in films. His fist didn't seem to move more than 6 inches, landing with an audible 'tok'. And the men just stopped, and a second later fell down senseless.

Another thing that Sandy did was not give jankers. All other sergeants and corporals would get you painting stones white or sweeping the parade ground or cleaning the latrines. Not Sandy.

"Follow me," he would rumble, crooking his finger to a wayward private. He would walk them behind the stables, they would hear 'tok' and then Sandy would come back.

"He won't do that again," and the matter was closed.

Sandy was a good friend to have, especially in a fight.

This was in direct contract to CSM Crisp, who was a cunt.

Most sergeants have authority as part of their personality, and can get soldiers to do what they require without screaming or threatening. Sadly Crisp was not one. His tenuous hold on his authority was maintained by spite, punishment and fear. Luckily for him, that army generally approves of this.

It had all started out, well enough, with Crisp shouting at Giles, no more and no less than he did with every other soldier.

Then, one day, Giles was in the company clerk's office, when a letter arrived.

"Fuckin' 'ell. 'Ere, read this," said the clerk handing Giles a letter. It was a letter addressed to the Commanding Officer from the London Police.

"What is it?"

"It's a letter saying that Crisp was arrested at Kings Cross for trying to have it off wiv' a twelve-year-old girl. The cunt's a kiddie fiddler.

Given the Sergeant's position, the Superintendent has decided not to take action at this time. Fuck me. They're lettin' 'im off 'cos he's an NCO."

"Christ! Crisp is a paedophile," said Giles, scanning the letter, not noticing the clerk's eyes flashing a warning.

"Reading confidential letters, private Holtom?" said a voice behind him. Crisp reached round and took the letter from his hands.

After a glance, he said, "If ever I hear you've spoken about this to anyone, I'll fuckin' crucify you. I'll make sure you wish you was dead.

You know, it seems to me that you don't have enough shit in your life. So I'm going to make sure your life is full of shit so you don't have time to read other people's letters. You can start by cleaning the barrack square and training grounds. Pick up all the horse shit, now – and use your hands. I don't want you to use a shovel. At the fuckin' double!"

So Giles had met his nemesis, and his name was Company Sergeant Major Crisp, the paedophile.

Now for Giles, the veterinary corps wasn't the easy billet that he thought it would be. The Household Cavalry specifically wanted a farrier, and this was his skill, but the Veterinary corps wanted soldiers who were Vets, surgeons, doctors, pharmacists, radiologists, horse and dog trainers, as well as being farriers.

Now, this being the British army, meant both lots of rote book learning and shovelling horse shit. Along with this, the animals had to be looked after, fed, watered and trained.

One of Giles' first jobs was the Monday morning dog clinic.

The army were given many dogs by the public. One person's "He's uncontrollable," was perfect for the army's needs and they took every dog given to them. Nowadays, some dog specialist has decided that all dogs have to be a Malinois but back then the RAVC accepted anything, collies, setters, Alsatians, boxers. The more vicious the better.

The dogs were then assigned a trainer who would assess their capabilities. Could they be trained for use, or were they just psychotic? They were given a week and the report was presented on the Friday, and it then became Giles' job in the Monday morning clinic, to euthanise those dogs that didn't make the cut.

The final part of his training was to be able to ride a horse.

Given that he had been riding in one form or another for most of his life, Giles thought that this might be the easy part. It wasn't.

He was being taught how to ride, the army way. Which is to say the cavalry way. He had to be able to ride at the same level as the (very few) cavalry units. Into the valley of death, and all that.

Step 1. Sit on your horse. Well surely this was easy. Each day, Giles was given a pair of short sticks. He had to place them between his knees and the flanks of this horse, and keep them there – for the whole day whilst riding bareback. First you started with holding your arms out at right angles to your body and then leaning back until your head touched the horse's rump. Then to sit up, and lean forward so that your forehead touched the horse's neck – holding on, just by gripping with your knees. Then you would go for a walk, trot, canter and gallop around the fields, whilst jumping over ditches, gates and logs. At the end of the day, he would hand back the sticks to the sergeant, and if a rider couldn't, then he was on jankers, and had to do the whole day's training again, until he could do it successfully.

Step 2. Move about the horse. Now that he could successfully sit on the horse, he was trained to be able to move around it. The original equipment to help with this training was the pommel horse. Yes. It was originally used to simulate a standing horse, to allow a cavalry rider to be able to move about the animal. Having mastered this on the pommel horse, it was time to move onto the real thing.

Thus Giles would be able to place two hands on the horse's back and swing his legs around the rump and over the neck. He would be able to spin and face backwards, to do a handstand, ride sitting on the rump, etc. He was expected to perform all of these tricks whilst the horse was cantering.

Then he was taught how to run alongside the horse at a gallop, holding onto its withers, to take giant steps every 5 yards to match the horse's pace. Then to be able to use his momentum to vault over the horse and land on the other side, still running.

Finally, he would be able to lean off the horse and pick up a handkerchief off the ground whilst galloping.

Ok. The circus tricks were over. He could handle a horse.

Step 3. Now it was time for spears! A proper cavalry officer had a lance, and his horse and body control were such that he could stick a lance point through a 1.5-inch (4cm) ring whilst bouncing in the saddle, at full gallop, leaning off his horse, holding on just with his knees.

Another thing they had to practise was using a lance to stick and pick up pegs knocked into the ground. The pegs were about 12 inches long by 1.5 inch wide (25cn x 4cm).

Yes. Once the army had finished with him, Giles could ride a horse, properly, like a cavalryman.

After about 9 months, Giles' 'basic' training was complete and the army considered him capable to be let out in public.

5. YOU'RE GOING ON A LITTLE HOLIDAY.

"Holtom, you're going on a little holiday."

"Yes, Sergeant."

"Take this 'orse to be x-rayed at St Thomas' Hospital, London."

By the '50's x-ray usage was relatively common, but machines were still big, bulky and expensive. Certainly, the RAVC wouldn't have one, but on occasion, required usage and give the size of the patients, they required specialist machines, and the only one in Britain that could film a horse was in St Thomas' (Guys) hospital at Waterloo, London.

Jolly got a horse box and pool car and dutifully set off for London. Given that it was Crisp that had sent him, he thought this was going to be a punishment, but it was turning out to be a bit of a fun trip out. Drive to London, x-ray the hose, come back. Piece of cake.

" 'scuse me constable. Which way to Guys hospital?" Jolly asked at a set of lights.

"Foller the signs for Westminster, turn left and look for signs to Waterloo, over the bridge."

Easy.

And it was. He made great time and was quickly parked round

the back of the hospital in an ambulance bay.

"'scuse me. Which way to x-ray?"

"End of the corridor. What the f.. Where are you takin' that 'orse?"

"x-ray."

"No, you bleedin' ain't."

"I have a special dispensation and orders. Here." Giles proffered the documents.

"Ho, yus, I fort so." Opined the doorman. "That's the teachin' section. Round the back. Service lift. Fifth floor."

Fifth floor! All of a sudden, this was turning out to be a little harder than expected.

Actually, it wasn't that bad and Giles soon had the horse into the small service lift, climbing up to the fifth floor. When the door opened, things became a bit more difficult.

Hospitals aren't built for horses to be able to wander through the halls, and this was even worse in the teaching part of the hospital, away from the wide corridors and wards.

The lift was big enough to fit 6 people, if they were friends, and it wasn't big enough for the horse to turn round, so Giles had to back him out into a narrow corridor.

People came round the corner, took one look at Giles and the horse and turned tail. It was even worse for people coming from the opposite direction, as they turned a corner and bumped into a horse's backside.

After much coaxing, swearing, nurses' squeals and neighs, the horse was delivered to the x-ray room at the far corner of the building.

It soon became apparent why they were using this machine, as it was the only one in Britain that could be manoeuvred to take films of such a large animal. And in fact, the x-ray part only took a couple of minutes.

"Now if you would mind getting that animal out of my hospital," said a doctor, and Giles set about retracing his steps, but given that the room and corridors were not big enough for the horse to turn round (or for Giles to get past), the whole procedure had to be done backwards. Cue more squeals, squeaks, neighs and swearing.

Eventually, Giles got the horse back to the lift and then downstairs and back in the horse box. After an uneventful drive, Giles arrived back at camp.

"You took your time, didn't you, Holtom?" smirked Crisp.

"Traffic, Sergeant," replied Giles, innocently.

It was only a few weeks before Giles was invited to take another holiday.

"Holtom, take these two dogs to Klagenfurt."

"Yes, sergeant," said Giles, and he shot off to the clerk's office to find a map. It was in Styria, Austria.

"Corp', can you get me to Klagenfurt?"

"There's no planes goin' there 'cos the Russians don't like it. We can fly you into Germany and then you'll have to find your own way. There'll be lots of trucks goin' to Austria. 'ere's a travel chitty and your orders."

It was 1950 and Giles learned that Austria was actually occupied by the Americans, the French, the British and the Russians. Just like Berlin, but a whole country. For him to get to Klagenfurt in the South, he would have to cross the Soviet, American and

French sectors.

Actually, it wasn't that hard, and after a flight to Frankfurt, he and the dogs had made their way down to Southern Germany, and then managed to hop onto a truck going to the British sector.

Now would be the time to tell lots of stories about daring runs under the cover of darkness, avoiding Russian patrols, but in fact, nothing more exciting happened than the swapping of cigarettes at check points.

"Holtom, Sir, and your two dogs," said Giles as he arrived at Klagenfurt.

"Jolly good. Find yourself a billet and we'll sort you out a bit of food once you've got them in the kennels."

And that was followed by a week in sunny, beautiful Styria, but all good things come to an end and Giles was called to see the CO.

"Do you ride?" he asked.

"Yes sir."

"Jolly good. I wonder if you could do me a favour on your way back. An old pal of mine, Joseph, is billeted in Vienna with the Hofreitschule."

"Sir?"

"The Spanish Riding School. They're quite famous you know." Giles didn't.

"He's usually based at the stud just down the road in Piber, but he's been moved up to the main school in Vienna. Anyway, if you would be kind enough to deliver this package to him, I would be very grateful." Giles nodded dumbly.

"Jolly good. I've amended your orders here, telling to you report to Vienna on urgent army business. Say 'Hello' to Joseph for me," he said passing over the orders and travel pass.

"Oh, by the way, it's in the international sector, so keep your head down. There's a good chap." The interview was ended and Giles was on his way to Vienna.

Austria and Vienna had been partitioned, but the city centre (the innere ring) was designated an international sector, patrolled jointly by all of the occupying powers. It was 1950, and just a year after the release of the hit film, "The Third Man", which was set in the international sector of Vienna, portraying a dark and brooding city, a pre-cursor for the cold war.

Into this stepped Giles, with his letter of introduction and package for Joseph Holböck.

The Hofreitschule, Michaelerplatz, Vienna, was unlike anything that he had ever seen before. "We ain't in Gainsford End now, Toto," Giles muttered as he looked at the massive baroque palace in front of him.

It was a contradiction, looking like an overblown, heavily iced wedding cake, but with the unmistakeable smell of horse manure.

Inside, after lots of hand waving, Giles was shown into the office of the Colonel in charge of the School. He didn't speak English and Giles didn't speak German. But things made a positive change when the Colonel called in Leutnant Holböck, who, it turned out, spoke excellent English, with a refined Austrian accent.

"So, vy are you here?" he asked.

"The Captain over at Klagenfurt asked me to deliver this," said Giles handing over the parcel.

"hmm, he says zat you are a Hufschmied. A black schmidt?"

"Yes, part of the British Army Veterinary Corps."

"Here ve have 85 horses and no proper Hufschmied. Zey did not come back from ze var. Perhaps, you can help us. Ja?"

And pretty much that was it. The Captain had sent him over with orders to help out, 'until relieved', and it was in fact the perfect job for him. He was working with the other School riders and staff, given a stipend to live on, and a place to stay.

His normal day, was the same as the staff, rising early, having breakfast, and then walking the 2km from their barracks to the Hofreitschule, where in the mornings he would inspect the horses, making a plan for any work that day, and then in the afternoon he was left to his own devices, but pretty soon, he was invited to participate in the horse riding and training.

"You can ride, ja?"

"Ja," said Giles, who by now had gained a certain level of soldier German. He couldn't form a sentence, but had lots of vocabulary necessary to his work; heiß, Kalt, druckig, schuh, eisen, essen, etc. Each, linked with a pointed finger, usually got what he needed.

"So, you ride like an Engländer, but now ve teach you Austrian equitation."

For those who don't know, the Hofreitschule (Spanish Riding School) is over 400 years old and is the only place where they practised Haute École, which is basically a style of high-level equestrianism and horse control from the renaissance period. Most people, know it for the dancing white Lipizzaner horses.

And so, days, weeks and months passed by. Giles was perfectly happy, living an idyllic, calm and quiet life. He was almost totally autonomous, with no sergeants or officers to bother him, and lots of time to indulge himself and hone his skills.

And then, one day, two British MPs turned up at the riding school, and took him away. The British Army had found him.

He was taken to British headquarters, where he was marched in front of a lieutenant and accused of being AWOL.

"It says here that you have been missing for 6 months," said the lieutenant.

"Yes, sir."

"Why?"

"Well, I was waiting for further orders. I had been told to stay until relieved." Said Giles, passing over his documentation.

"Yeeeeees," drawled the lieutenant. "We shall have to see about that. In the meantime, there are a couple of chaps outside, who want a quick word with you."

Giles was marched out, to be confronted by a couple of men in grey overcoats.

"If you wouldn't mind following us, old chap. We have a couple of questions we would like you to answer." And he was escorted out of the building and into the back of a waiting black Opel sedan, where he was whisked away to another part of the city.

There were two of them.

"Now, Private Holtom, my name is Captain Brown and this is my colleague, er, Captain Brown."

"Sugar?" asked Captain Brown solicitously, handing Giles a cup of tea, and then, "It seems that you have been living here in Vienna, in the international sector, whilst embedded with the Austrian Army. Correct?"

In the international sector, which was the central part of Vienna, all four powers had equal sway, as opposed to the sectors that they controlled outright. Because no one power had jurisdiction, it was the norm, for 4 soldiers, one from each power, to travel around in jeeps together. They would police the public, and depending upon who/what they found would defer to one or another's authority, for example, if they suspected someone of selling black market goods, and his papers said he was Polish, then the Russians would take control, etc.

Vienna was also a crossing point from East to West and vice versa, and rather like Casablanca, it was famous for spies. On top of this, the Americans and the British were spying on the Russians, and the Russians in turn on the Americans and British. The French spied on the British. Nobody knew why.

And so the questions began. It seems that the Captains Brown were highly interested in what Giles had managed to see, overhear and learn during his sojourn. Whilst it had not directly affected him this was a very turbulent time in Austria. In fact the place was riven with strikes and factionalist violence, mostly between Austria communists and the rest of the populace.

The British, French and Americans had actually started to stockpile weapons to give to the Austrian Police and former army personnel, in preparation for a potential civil war. But they held back. Neither Russia, nor the allies wanted Austria to erupt into war. They were all worried that Austria might become Europe's Korean war.

And so, Giles had to answer questions on popular feeling and political opinion on the ground, the state of readiness to attack each other, the availability of weapons, etc.

In the end, he was received his documents back and given a lift back to the British barracks.

"There'll be no problem with your little stay. I'll have a word with your CO, but we suggest that you hop off home, sharpish. There's a good chap."

And so, Giles jumped onto a truck heading to Germany, and then back to Melton Mowbray.

"You are so fucked," bawled Crisp. "you are goin' to spend the rest of your fuckin' service in Colchester." Colchester Camp was the Army's prison barracks.

But, when Giles was paraded in front of Lieutenant Spurry, all Crisp heard was, "I just had a chat with a Captain Brown and it seems the Private Holtom was doing something at the request of the locals, and that we can't talk about it. So, there's an end to it. Nice to have you back Holtom."

"Yes sir," said both Giles, smiling and Crisp, scowling.

Meanwhile in the news:

Daily Mail
Horse in Hospital Lift. Photo page 3.

Wiener Zeitung
Hofreitschule to open as they find new Hufschmied

6.   A SOLDIER GOES TO WAR.

Having been away for nearly 8 months, Giles had actually earned some furlough, and he was given a week's leave.

He travelled up to Scarborough, where his mother, Hilda, had set up with her new husband Larry. The had bought a house and ran it as a boarding house. When Giles was there it was summer season, and he and his brother Derek had to sleep in the garden shed, as all rooms were taken.

One girl who was staying there with her family was Elizabeth. She was 17 and he was 18, and in the way of things in those days, they went out for a couple of walks, and got on well. Maybe she was impressed by his dashing good looks and stories of Vienna. In any case, at the end of the week, they decided to write to each other.

Giles returned to Barracks, to see CSM Crisp beaming across his face. This didn't bode well.

"You've 'ad yer fuckin' 'oliday. Now it's time for you to go to war, soldier.
This ain't no leisurely trip to Germany. Oh no. You are off to fuckin' Korea.
Be packed and ready for departure tomorrow at 0600."

"Balls," thought Giles.

And so, early the next morning he, two other privates and corporal Elvin jumped into the back of a Lorry, and went off to war.

The first part of the trip was basically the boat train, and then on to Paris, where they changed onto a sleeper train to Trieste. Once in Trieste, they were scheduled to take a ship down the Adriatic to Cyprus, where they would meet up with the troop ship taking them to Korea.

All, went well, with a couple of leisurely days looking out of the carriage windows at France, Germany and Austria as they rolled past. Then Yugoslavia, and finally to arrive in Italy.

On the last morning on the train, after the checkpoint crossing for Yugoslavia, they were told by the conductor that the next stop was Trieste, and to get ready. They had plenty of time, so Giles went off to the bathroom to have a wash and a shave, leaving the others in the sleeping cabin.

As he was finishing up, he noticed that the train was slowing down. They were stopping!

"Kerrist," swore Giles, as he towelled off his face and ran along the corridor back to the compartment, only to find it empty. His companions had gone, and so were their packs. His own kitbag was sitting alone on his bed.

Grabbing the bag, his uniform jacket and hat, he bolted along the corridor, just as the train ground and hissed to a halt. Giles hopped off, onto the platform and looked up and down for his colleagues.

Around him, was a deserted platform. Nothing. Nobody. Shit.

Maybe the station had platforms both sides. Some stations that had stopped at were like that. Giles crouched down to look under the carriage to see it he could see anything on the other side. Still nothing.

So, he adjusted his jacket and hat, shouldered his kitbag and started to walk along the carriages, just as the train shuddered, hissed and lurched into motion.

It shouldn't do that. This was the end of the line.

And then, as the train gathered speed, Giles looked up at the carriages as they went past, and saw his colleagues, sitting in the restaurant car, having their breakfasts, looking down, open mouthed at him, standing on the platform. Bugger.

He had got off at the stop which wasn't a stop. He was in Yugoslavia.

Not only that, but he was a British army soldier in Yugoslavia, which for the last 5 years had been behind the iron curtain. Technically, he was in enemy territory.

As the train disappeared into the distance, he noticed a little man looking at him from a hut on the other side of the tracks. He had a uniform of sorts and Giles guessed the he was the station master.

He had to find a way to get out of here.

Strolling over to the hut, the man seemed puzzled rather than scared that he was being approached by a British soldier. And then it struck Giles that the veterinary corps' uniform didn't look like a normal British soldier.

It was all very formal and turn of the century, based on cavalry and horse riding. In fact, the uniform he had been issued with, was stamped 1916 inside on the label. The army didn't throw stuff away. Anyway, he had a peaked cap, rather than a beret, knee length riding boots and jodhpurs rather than army boots and baggy trousers. For all the world he looked like a German officer, except they wore field grey and he was field green, - just like, wait a minute, Yes. Just like a Russian officer.

Maybe this was his way out, he thought. This was Yugoslavia. They would know Russian officers but probably not speak Russian.

"Don't you know to salute an officer?" said Giles in his best Essex/Russian twang.

"Kto si?"

"Me, Russkie Officier. Yes?" shouted Giles. "Trieste." He said, pointing at his chest. "Trieste."

"Zavolám políciu," the man replied, reaching for the phone.

"Exactly. Chop."

30 minutes later a small 2-stroke car warbled into view, surrounded by a cloud of blue smoke. In it was a policeman.

Everybody was very jolly and nice, but Giles was arrested.

"Me, Russkie. Trieste." Said Giles.

In turn they nodded, and said, "Trieste."

They smiled, patted his arm and pushed him into the car, and after a 10-minute drive, they arrived at a tiny village, reminiscent of Gainsford End, and he was shown into a cell in the police house. He was a prisoner.

It wasn't all bad. They left the cell door open. It was time to make plans.

Giles decided that, if they continued to leave the cell door open then he would sneak out in the middle of the night and head across country to Trieste. Richard Hannay had nothing on him. There was even a map on the police office wall, so he could check out a route.

Just so long as they didn't decide to question him in the meantime. Did that mean cattle prods and brass knuckles? Bloody hell, he hoped not.

Just then the door to the cells opened, and Giles held his breath.

A young girl, maybe about 10 years old, came into the cell carrying a tray of food. She put it down by Giles' side, on his bed, and settled herself onto the opposite bunk, to watch him. So, no cattle prods then.

He imagined they didn't get many Russian Officers coming through here.

The food was like nothing that he had ever seen before. It was some kind of vegetable. They were red and green, and stuffed with meat and rice. Giles had never seen peppers before. Anyway, they tasted just fine, and they were covered in a kind of tomato sau. sau.., sau…. Wow! This wasn't like any kind of tomato sauce he had ever tasted. It nearly took the top of his head off, much to the amusement of the watching girl.

She pointed, helpfully at a glass jug which seemed to contain some kind of squash. He drank down a whole glass in one go, and the burning eventually subsided.

This just left a small glass of clear liquid, which after a quick smell, he was unsure if it was to drink or to clean the toilets. He had never had plum brandy before.

After the meal, the girl left, taking the tray with her, but leaving the cell door open.

That evening, after another meal of strange, but tasty food, Giles banged his head twice on his pillow. He would wake up at 0200 and then he would be miles away by dawn.

He was woken, after a pleasant night's sleep, at 8am, by the little girl coming back with breakfast. So much for escaping. Maybe he wasn't cut out to be a John Buchan character.

The breakfast consisted of a bowl of some kind of buttermilk with the consistency of thick custard. They served it with a spoonful of honey drizzled on top. It was delicious, and when he finished it, the girl took the bowl away and returned with a refill.

The tray also held a hunk of brown bread, some black coffee that tasted like road planings, and another glass of the plum rocket fuel.

When breakfast was finished, the policeman came in and, through the use of hand signals, asked Giles to follow him.

"Trieste," he said, pointing at Giles' chest.

They set off in the little car, bouncing over the small roads to the next village. After some waving and pointing, Giles learned that the car was called a Trabant and that it was made out of papier mâché or something similar. The engine seemed to be a very low tuned 2-stroke that belched clouds of blue smoke out of the back.

Giles noticed that there was no rear-view mirror and concluded that it would be useless as all the driver could see would be smoke.

After about 30 minutes, they arrived at another small village, where the policeman took Giles' kitbag out of the car, and handed him over to an old farmer.

"Trieste," he said pointing at the farmer and then to Giles. Then he waved cheerily and drove off.

The farmer put the kitbag into the back of a cart, and beckoning Giles to follow, hopped up on the front.

"Russkie. Trieste," said Giles by way of explanation. The old man nodded and they moved off.

The rest of the day was spent meandering, at a slow walk, from farm to farm, as the farmer delivered and picked up different vegetables and sacks of produce.

One of the most amazing things that Giles noticed was that the horses were not shod using iron but rather rubber cut out from old car tyres. The horse would walk along the tarmac in eery silence.

That evening was spent in a farm house, where, after dinner, the farmer beckoned Giles to follow him and walked up stairs. In the back bedroom he pulled away a blanket to reveal an old WW2 British army radio.

It was exactly like the one Giles had used in basic training.

"visky, tango forty-nine," said the farmer, pointing at his chest. "visky, tango forty-nine." It seems that the old farmer had been a partisan fighting against the Nazis and that he had been supplied by the British. And so, they spent the evening, drinking home-made plum brandy, and talking, each in their own language, about the war.

Early the next morning, Giles was woken with breakfast. He learned that the buttermilk stuff was called yaourt. And he especially liked it spread with honey onto the heavy brown bread. He was even getting used to the plum brandy.

"Trieste."

"Trieste," replied Giles, and they hopped into a lorry.

The drive took a couple of hours, winding through small roads and smaller hamlets, until finally they came to a halt at a junction.

The driver got out and walked to the corner, looking around the edge of the building. Ducking back out of sight, he gestured for Giles to join him. They both peeked around the corner and Giles could see, 50 yards away, a sentry box, a red and white striped barrier and a border guard.

"Trieste," said the old man, pointing past the guard.

They shook hands, and Giles slung his kitbag over his shoulder.

"Good Luck, Tommy," said the farmer, as he turned and walked away.

Meanwhile in the news:

Daily Mail
Army returns from successful incursion behind Iron Curtain

Правда
Glorious Third Division successfully repels sneak attack by capitalist NATO forces.

Halstead Gazette
Be very careful of spicy tomatoes, but brandy made from Plums is good, reports Private Giles Holtom. Police report increase in scrumping.

7.   MEN IN GREY COATS

Giles was walking the 50 yards from the corner to the border control.

"Good luck, Tommy?"

This meant that they had known he was a British soldier all along. And they had helped him anyway.

It also explained the playing with British Army radio sets and the tortuous route through the back roads, missing towns (and most likely Police and checkpoints).

Well, he obviously wasn't cut out for espionage or a life like Dick Barton, but they had helped him, and here he was, walking to the border crossing to Trieste.

When he was 10 yards away from the border guard, Giles snapped a salute and held it as he walked on. The soldier wasn't sure who this was. He wasn't a Yugoslav officer, but who was he? Russian, maybe? In any case, his training kicked in and he shouldered his rifle and returned the salute.

Giles walked up to the guard, and in one quick movement, side-stepped him and ducked under the barrier, and ran like hell.

The 30 yards or so to the Italian barrier seemed like miles and all of the time Giles was expecting to be shot in the back.

The soldier didn't fire. Maybe he was in shock. Maybe he didn't want to fire toward the Italian side. Who knows, but he didn't shoot, and Giles ducked under the Italian barrier.

He was finally safe.

"Well, what do we have here?" said an American voice. It seems that the border was guarded by Americans as well as Italians.

"Been to see your Comrades, huh?"

"I am a British soldier," puffed Giles.

"Yeah. Well it looks like you just been to see your Komisar, buddy. Put your hands up." And so, Giles was arrested for the second time in 3 days, this time by the Americans, as a spy.

He was dragged off in the back of a jeep and taken to a building not far away, and was kept in a cell with an armed American MP guarding the door.

Despite being a real prisoner, the Americans treated him well, and after he was suspicious of local Italian food, "What is that?", the gave him steak and potatoes, which was the first steak he had had to eat since before the war.

For three days, American soldiers quizzed him about his exploits and how he had got there. Safe to say, they didn't really believe him. Who would? And then, on the morning of the 4th day, the door opened to reveal corporal Elvin from his unit.

"Yes, that's him," confirmed Elvin. "He was on the train with us, and got off at a halt a couple of hours before we reached Trieste."

It seemed that the Americans had contacted his unit in Cyprus to see if anyone could corroborate Giles' story, and they sent Elvin back to do this. The Americans handed Giles over to Elvin for transport back to his unit, and a court martial.

On leaving the building, Giles and Elvin were stopped by a couple of men in grey coats.

"Carry on Elvin. We will take care of things from here, there's a good chap," said Captain Brown, ushering Giles into a black sedan, which whisked him off into the city.

"Nice to see you again, private Holtom. We think, after your adventures, that you might have a little information that could be useful to us. You know the drill."

It turns out that no British soldier had been in Yugoslavia since 1945, and that as they were now behind the iron curtain, the Men in Grey were very interested in any information Giles could give them.

The Captains Brown wanted to know what arms the police used, etc. and Giles also told them about the cars, rubber horse shoes, transport, and food. They were especially interested in learning about 'visky Tango forty-nine' and his radio.

In fact, one Captain Brown left the room and returned a while later with the news that this was a valid call sign for a partisan soldier during the war.

"Maybe we should send a message via radio, telling him that the parcel had arrived in Trieste. Who knows, maybe he could give us some more information too."

And so it went on, for 2 days.

"Well, thank you for that, private," said Captain Brown, "hop on a boat down to Cyprus to re-join your chaps. I'll call your commanding officer to let him know you've been helping us. Cheerio."

Two days later Giles presented himself to the army depot in Cyprus, where he was met by a less than sanguine CSM Crisp.

"AWOL. Spying, and a court martial," he screamed. "and you get none of them because of some Army Intelligence fucker protect-

ing your arse. That doesn't mean that I can't make your life hell –
and I'm goin' to enjoy it."

Still, it wasn't all bad. The troop ship for Korea had already sailed
and Giles wasn't on it. He had missed going to the war.

∞

Let's fast forward to a regimental reunion in the '70's, where
Giles was stopped by a guy seated at a table near him.

"Holtom?" he said.

"Yes," replied Giles, not recognising the man. "Do I know you?"

"No, we never met, but I fuckin' hate you."

"Oh?" said Giles, nonplussed.

"I was keepin' my 'ead down in Cyprus in 1950, all nice and quiet
like, when you didn't turn up to take your berth on the troop ship
to Korea. They sent me instead. I was there 2 ½ years! I fuckin'
hate you."

Giles could empathise, and said he was sorry. In fact, after they
had had a drink together, all seemed to be forgiven. It's amazing
what 20 years distance will do.

Meanwhile in the news:

New York Times
Rationing in the UK; Brit soldier never had steak before.

Variety

Kowalski captures Komisar
from clutches of Krauts.

Daily Mail

English spies are the best. Photo page 3.

Halstead Gazette

American steaks are great, says
Giles, but beware Italian food.

8.   COURT MARTIAL AT WADI YERWANNA

ell, Giles had missed getting court martialled, but it wasn't going to be long in coming.

W

"Over 'ere Holtom," bawled Crisp. "I've got another little job for you – Addis Ababa in Ethi-fuckin'-opia."

Giles marched over to the company clerk's office to receive his orders and travel permits, and more importantly to look at a map. Where the hell was Ethiopia?

The first part was easy and Giles hopped in a transport to Moascar/Ismailia on the Suez canal. Moascar was the remount centre for the army, with several RAVC being posted there.

From there, Giles couldn't get a boat down the red sea, but managed to hitch a lift in the back of a platoon's transport going to Southern Egypt. This took 3 days driving, a large part of which was across the desert, before they arrived at a small camp set up at the mouth of a wadi.

"'oo the 'ell are you?" asked the sergeant as he counted his men off the back of the trucks.

"Holtom, veterinary corps, sergeant. I was hitching a lift with your lads on my way to Ethiopia."

"You'd better come with me, son."

And so, Giles found himself in front of a slightly sandy and dishevelled Captain of the Royal Leicestershire regiment.

"This is a bit of luck, and you might be able to help us out a bit," said the captain. "My men are engaged in a small action about 2 miles up the wadi, and I need someone to manage the mules used to deliver water supplies to the men. That's a job for the veterinary corps, isn't it?"

"Er, yes, sir," admitted Giles.

"Good chap. It'll only be for a day or two. Keep your head down."

And so, Giles was put in charge of 4 mules carrying jerry cans of water up through the wadi to the Leicestershire's.

This was a simply stroll up the dried river bed for 2 miles, all the while, he could hear the occasional, sporadic rifle boom and crack echo down the wadi towards him.

He turned a corner and came across a platoon of soldiers, about 100 yards in front of him. They were all sitting in fox holes, with their heads down. 200 yards in front of them was an escarpment, and Giles could see some tribesmen on the top looking down at him. It seems as though the Leicestershire's had got themselves pinned down.

Hmmm. This required thinking about and so he parked the mules behind some rocks and scrub and sat to study the situation.

He had to deliver water across the open wadi bed to the soldiers in their fox holes. Presumably, all the time, he would be in the open and being fired upon by the tribesmen on the escarpment. Given the choice, he would rather be in Bognor.

Giles had quite a bit of experience shooting, both from the farm and his basic training (where he had scored well). He was used to handling the Army issue Enfield .303. With a proficient shooter it was a good gun, and reasonably accurate up to 300 yards. He was accurate up to about 200 yards. But in most cases, with open sights and in the hands of less skilled shooters, 100 yards was a better maximum range.

At the same time, the tribesmen probably didn't have Enfields. He had seen several, sitting on their camels, on his journey down from Moascar, and their armaments ranged from pre-WW1 Martini Henry single action rifles, down to wheel lock rifles, which were at best ornamental antiques.

So, even though it was dangerous, the odds were that nobody would be able to reliably hit a man standing up, whilst firing downhill and at a range of over 200 yards. At least he hoped so.

In any case, the odds were a damn sight better than those for his grandad, as he walked over no man's land in the Somme.

And so, Giles formulated a plan. He would carry 2 jerry cans across the open area and deliver to two fox holes at a time, jumping into the second one for cover. The tribesmen would probably only have time to get in a ranging shot before he was out of sight. He would wait a minute or so and then leg it back to the mules for more jerries.

On the first trip, the tribesmen were so surprised that they didn't fire at all. They all sat up and watched as Giles scuttled from fox hole to fox hole, bemused.

The same thing happened with his second sortie. They simply watched him. Who was this mad man?

On the third trip, they fired a couple of shots at him. Whether it was to try and hit him or just to make him run faster, he didn't know – but it worked. He dived into the second fox hole, landing on top of a private.

"Sorry mate."

"No. You carry on, lad," said a lilting Welsh voice. "We appreciate the water, see."

"I think I'll stop here for a second and have a fag. Got any?"

And so, a quiet 5 minutes passed before Giles scrambled back to the mules.

This carried on for nearly an hour, during which time, he had delivered water to 16 soldiers and their lieutenant. He had been shot at about 5 times, but no bullets had struck closer than 5 yards to him, and so, he walked back down the wadi to the camp.

The following day, Giles made the same trip twice, in the morning and late afternoon.

His arrival would generate a stir of excitement on the top of the escarpment, and a couple of men would sit down, and try to shoot him. Giles figured that they were probably betting on the outcome. It was something to break the boredom.

When he left, they stood up and cheered him, waving good bye until his next visit.

So for two days, Giles delivered water to the stalemate. The platoon pinned down under the escarpment and the tribesmen sitting on the top. He guessed that the lieutenant had missed class they day they taught outflanking.

On the morning of the third day, they had got close with a couple of shots hitting about a yard from his feet, and so he picked up his pace and dived into the last fox hole.

"Your dwawing fire, you bloody man," squeaked the lieutenant. The tension making his voice raise an octave and double in volume.

"It's me they're shooting at, you one-pip wonder. Not you," said an aggrieved Giles.

There was a stifled guffaw from the next fox hole, and the lieutenant piped, "I'll have you bloody well court martialled. You insubordinate swine. Follow me back to camp."

And so, Giles was dragged before the Captain.

"I want this man court martialled for insubordination and insolence, sir," said the Lieutenant, having regained his composure.

"Yes. I see that, Pratt, but he was actually delivering water to your troops. If he hadn't done this, whilst being shot at, I might add, then you wouldn't have been able to continue your action. In fact, my reports tell me that Private Holtom acted very bravely under fire. It is suggested that he gets a commendation."

"But sir," said Pratt, "I can't have my authowity questioned in fwont of my men."

And so it was, that Giles was both put forward for a court martial and recommended for a medal, both from the same action.

A couple of hours later the platoon arrived back in camp.

It seems that when the lieutenant had left, the sergeant had moved the men to flank the escarpment. They arrived at the top to find that the tribesmen had disappeared, and so had returned to camp.

Thus ended the battle of wadi yerwanna makethoseeyes atmifor.

"in my report, I've ordered that the court martial is dismissed. You won't have to worry about that," said the Captain the next day, as Giles prepared to leave. He also arranged for a truck to give him a lift to the nearest town, where he could make his own way on to Addis Ababa.

The captain left Giles with this thought, "Which way are you coming back from Addis? Only, I would advise you to seek out another route to this one. This was just a small skirmish, but I have a feeling that things are going to get a bit hotter in this region soon. Best avoid, eh."

◆ ◆ ◆

Fast forward 35 years to 1985, in Llandeilo. Giles was standing next to a guy looking down into a garage inspection pit, watching the mechanic work on his car.

Their conversation had meandered through cars, work and the weather, when Giles noticed a tattoo on his forearm. These were the days when tattoos were rare, and only generally found on sailors.

"What's that?"

"My regiment, boy. Royal Leicestershire Fusiliers."

"I did some work with them a long time ago."

"Really? What regiment were you in?"

"Veterinary corps."

"I've only ever met one guy from them. It was in 1950 in Sudan. He called Pratty, my lieutenant, a one-pip wonder."

"That was me."

"Really?"

"Yes. I was delivering water to some platoon."

"That was us. You jumped in my fox hole."

"Here's the cigarette I owe you."

Meanwhile in the news:

Daily Mail

Successful British action against
overwhelming native odds.

Halstead Gazette

Giles shot at; mentioned in dispatches.

9. LION AROUND IN ADDIS

"Holtom, sir," reported Giles, as he arrived at the British Embassy in Addis Ababa.

"Ah. Jolly good. We've been expecting you. They're waiting for you up at the Palace," said the official, and after glancing at Giles' travel-stained uniform, said, "Get yourself smartened up a bit before you go." And so, he found himself in the kitchens at the back of the embassy, having a wash, whilst some servant sponged down his kit.

And then, off to the Palace of His Imperial Majesty, Field Marshall Haile Selassie I, Emperor of Ethiopia, Conquering Lion of the Tribe of Judah. As a ruler, he could trace his lineage back, directly to Solomon and Sheba.

"Bloody hell. I wonder what they want me to do here," mused Giles as he drove thought the gates of the palace grounds.

"Lions," said the equerry a few minutes later.

"Lions?"

"Well one lion actually. You see, the emperor keeps several lions in the palace, as his pets. He is, after all, the Lion of Judah. Well, anyway, one of his pet lions seems to have a problem and we asked the British government if they could help with an expert, and they sent you."

"What kind of a problem?"

"Oh, the usual kind. He's started attacking people. He's killed three servants."

Giles cast his mind back to CSM Crisp leering at him as he'd been handed his orders. The bastard knew.

"How big is he?" asked Giles as he looked through the bars.

"Him big," said the keeper, "maybe 450 pounds. Him usually good cat. No problem. But now he angry."

On watching the lion for a while, Giles guessed that there was a problem with his mouth. Possibly an abscess or maybe a broken tooth. The one thing he was certain about was that he wasn't going to put his hand in the damned animal's mouth to find out.

"I need to send a telex. Take me to the office." And Giles scribbled a quick note to the Royal Veterinary College in London, asking how much Lidocaine to use to knock out a lion.

"Now we wait."

They had put him into a bungalow in the palace grounds. Under normal circumstances, he would consider it, well, palatial, and it was. Except for the lions freely walking around the grounds.

He had been told to come up to the back of the palace to be fed, but to do that, he would have to cross the compound.

He stepped out of the door and braced himself to start, when he looked to his left and saw an askari walking toward him along the path, and slap in the middle of it, sat a lion.

Giles' feet were frozen to the veranda and he couldn't move. Trying to appear nonchalant, he lit a cigarette with a shaking hand, as the askari walked round the lion and continued on his way. He gulped and stepped forward onto the path, scurrying after the askari, so he could walk with him. Maybe, if the lion attacked, he would eat him first, hoped Giles.

At night, they lit torches on the paths, so Giles could see his way home to his bungalow. Once inside, he noticed that it seemed to be constructed of what seemed like paper, and he could clearly see the shadow of a lion sitting on his veranda, through the wall.

He lay quietly on the bed, trying not to make a sound like a piece of meat.

In the morning, the RVC telex had come back. 1cc per 50 pounds weight.

And so, he set off with the keeper and an askari to put the lion into a cattle crush. Once installed, the lion couldn't move, and Giles prepared to inject it.

Now let's see, 450 pounds means 9cc. Hmmm. Better make it 18cc to be sure.

The way to check if an animal is 'out' is to open the eye and to touch the eyeball. If there is any kind of flinch, wait another few seconds, or in Giles' case, give it another couple of cc's. After another minute or two it was obvious from the snores, that the lion was completely asleep, and Giles began.

Actually draining an abscess and removing a molar only took about 15 minutes, and soon, everything was completed.

"Now, just keep checking his eyeball," Giles told the askari. "Tell me when he wakes up."

It took three days.

Which wasn't surprising, given the amount of Lidocaine Giles had given him. But on the third day, the lion woke up and they all stood around the cage watching as he came out of his stupor.

After 30 minutes of groggy stumbling the lion finally managed to get to his feet and he paced around.

"Try him with some food."

The askari threw in some meat, and after a quick sniff, the lion started to eat.

"He is well. He is well," chanted the keeper. "You save my lion. He is well."

There isn't much more to be said. The Palace was happy, and it was arranged to give him transport to help him get home. Mindful of the Captain's advice, he asked to be dropped off South, in Kenya, rather than make his way back North, though Sudan.

And so, after hitching his way through Kenya, Uganda, the Congo and Nigeria, he got passage on a ship out of Lagos, bound for the Mediterranean, and eventually, Cyprus.

"Holtom reporting, sir."

"Lieutenant Spurry wants to see you, and don't think I don't know about the court martial. I've made sure it's marked down on your record," growled Crisp.

"Holtom reporting, sir," this time to lieutenant Spurry.

"Ah, Holtom. Nice to have you back from your travels. It appears that you have had a couple of scrapes, eh. Well, the good news is that the court martial has been waived, and the better news is that you have been nominated for a commendation. I've also got a telegram from the Embassy in Ethiopia. It seems that the Emperor is very happy with your work, and his ambassador extends his thanks to you and to the British Army. Hmmm," said Spurry, "You have been busy haven't you."

"In the meantime, there's a Captain Brown who would like a word with you. He asked you to drop down to the base at Akrotiri to see him."

Meanwhile in the news:

Daily Telegraph
Emperor Hailie Selassie sends Lion to Queen Elizabeth as gesture of thanks and friendship.

Daily Mail
Hunt for missing Corgi at palace. Photo page 3.

10.   CRETE

"They are lookin' for a Rabies expert, an' I have decided that means you," said CSM Crisp. "So read up about it, an' don't get bitten."

In 1950 Rabies, also called hydrophobia, was an incurable disease. Once contracted, it was invariably fatal. Before 2016, there have only been 14 cases of a human surviving rabies. It could be caught by contact from a rabid animal. A bite, or even a lick to an open cut.

There had been trials of a new vaccine, but nobody knew if it had worked. Rabies can only be diagnosed once the symptoms have started and the vaccine is only effective if administered before symptoms appear. So, the only way to tell if someone had had the disease and recovered, was an autopsy. If you died, you had it. If you lived, the vaccine might have worked, or you simply might not have had it in the first place.

Giles was being sent to Crete to clear the island of rabid dogs. He guessed that CSM Crisp was hoping that he would get bitten.

The process was quite straightforward. The local police put up posters explaining that all dogs, without a collar, were to be destroyed on a particular date, and the populace had to put a collar on their dogs if they wanted them to be safe.

As the date arrived, Giles with help from the police and some army, started at one end of the island and worked their way to the other, collecting dogs as they advanced.

It isn't a nice job.

Most of the feral dogs were snappy and aggressive when cornered. They had learned to expect nothing but kicks and thrown stones from the people of the island. Some were strangely calm and friendly, but this was even more scary, as at one stage of the disease, infected animals can lose all fear of humans. This is why it is very scary when little kids playing in the gardens come across seemingly wild animals that approach and are friendly.

The best way to catch the dogs was to corner them and use a long pole with a noose on the end. The dog could be held still whilst Giles euthanised them with an injection, all the while avoiding being bitten or licked by the dogs. Some dogs were too smart, or too vicious to be caught with the noose and so had to be shot where they were caught.

The bodies were then thrown into the back of a truck behind them. Each evening, the bodies in the back of the lorry would be taken away and burned.

Every so often, a distraught dog owner would come out and try to interfere with the process, usually because they had completely ignored the instructions to put a collar onto their dogs.

And so, hour after hour, and day after day, for nearly a week, the line moved across the island, killing as they went.

On the fourth day, Giles was bitten.

The man holding the long pole had slipped and the dog had turned on Giles as he reached forward to inject it. It wasn't a big bite, nor was it that deep, but it was easily deep enough to kill him.

It was time to use the vaccine he had brought with him. He was driven back to his billet. The situation was that, he was on Crete a couple of days away from Cyprus, where his unit was based. There was no-one qualified to help him. He was on his own.

The vaccine was kept, cultured and incubated in test tubes filled with duck egg albumen and the treatment regime was a series of 12 daily injections directly into the abdomen.

Being the expert, and with no other person around who had the necessary knowledge, Giles would have to inject himself.

Now, even the bravest among us would have trouble doing this, and Giles wasn't that brave. But he also wasn't stupid. Rabies was fatal, and if he didn't vaccinate himself, then he would die.

"Bloody hell," he thought as he prepared his first dose. He was used to administering industrial sized injections into horses and dogs, but not humans, and certainly not into himself.

The technology at the time was using big bore needles which required a strong push to get them into and through the skin, compared to today's micro bore needles which often can't even be felt.

The needle was 4-5" (12-15cm) long and he had to pierce the skin, push though the abdominal muscles to the full depth of the needle and deliver the vaccine into his abdominal wall. One per day for 12 days.

Each day's injection left a halfpenny sized, red weal on his skin.

"I feel like a bloody dart board," he mused as he looked at this stomach, with its red bumps, describing a circle, like the numerals of a clock.

The days passed with him sitting in his billet, being fed food cooked by a local policeman's wife. They dropped in every day to see how he was, but mostly he supposed they really wanted to see if hair was growing on the back of his hands or any other signs that might mean he was infected and be turning into a wolf.

12 days later Giles released himself from quarantine.

The island was clear of rabies and he prepared to return to Cyprus.

"Oh, dear. What a pity," said CSM Crisp. It wasn't sure if he was commiserating about having been bitten or about having recovered.

"Still, you're back just in time for a little visit to Egypt."

Meanwhile in the news:

Halstead Gazette

Giles Holtom has rabies and is ordered
to keep away from dogs.

Veronica Mellis (nee Whitty) has twins. "Ginger hair can be a genetic trait," says Veronica.

Правда

The glorious Soviet Socialist Republic
reports that Rabies has been eliminated
by our brave leadership and
our countries do not have this
capitalism disease.

Variety

Kowalski's Kraut Komisar contracts
raging Rottweiler's Rabies.

11.   EGYPT

Initially, Giles was stationed at Moascar, which was an army remount centre and there were several RAVC stationed there, including Sandy, Sam Perrie and Jim Dobson, all of whom were friends of his.

Moascar is an area of Ismailia, which is a town on the banks of the Suez canal. Egypt was a nominally independent country but it was in fact under British military occupation until WW2.

In 1950, when Giles was there, the nationalist Wafd party had won a landslide victory with the premise of removing the British. In 1951, King Farouk ordered British troops out of the Suez. The British refused to leave, and the Egyptians cut off the water and food supplies to the camp. The King's government and later that of Gamal Abdel Nasser (who overthrew the King) promoted guerrilla activity against the British turning the area into a low-level war zone – but then Giles had already experienced this in his previous visit to Egypt.

The Suez canal itself, was the main artery for the transport of goods and people from East to West and vice versa. As a large amount of the goods were either to or from British interests, they wanted to ensure control of this vitally strategic route.

This is the situation in which Giles, and the rest of the Veterinary Corps found themselves. The Captain that he had met in Sudan, was right. This was going to turn out to be more than a small skirmish.

Well here he was in Egypt.

"Smells; that is something that most books and articles do not mention when writing about foreign countries, and they all seem to have their own," Giles once told me.

"I only have to smell something and it immediately reminds me of a country or place I have been in. Some are more exotic than others, though I think the first time you are away from home the more noticeable the smell is.

Nothing sticks in my mind like the smells on that first journey. Coming down through various European countries eventually to Egypt, I noticed that they all have their over-riding smell. These seem to stick in your mind and without them half the enjoyment of foreign places would be lost, at least for me it would. These smells don't have to be nasty or obnoxious, just different, and they are there in the back of your mind for ever.

One of the major smells for northern Europe seems to be very strong smoking tobacco, especially in France and their dark cigarettes, (and their open toilets). In North Africa it was spices, which is true of all of the east, though they seem to vary from place to place.

The same can be said of shoeing smoke, you only have to go near a person who has been shoeing and you know exactly what they do, it can't be hidden. Driving through the country you used to know when you were near a forge by that whiff of burnt hoof, and it still conjures-up the vision of the forge of my youth."

Before he had started Giles had to get a haircut. He set about finding the barber and after a few enquiries found that one came once a week to the unit, and as luck would have it this was the day he was there.

He was told to go round the back of the stables and to ask for Jock McGregor, quite expecting an ex-pat or retired serviceman, he was surprised to say the least, when he turned out to be a Berber tribesman complete with tribal scars, and as black as black can be. 'Jock' spoke with a very broad Scottish accent, and he first asked Giles if he ken Dundee of all places. He seemed quite surprised and disappointed when Giles said no.

A bit later while cutting his hair one of the boys walked by and said "Hello Jock, what did you have for breakfast?", evidently an on-going joke.

Anyway he answered much to Giles bemusement and surprise, "Bread and Butter and bloody hot water, not a bit of good, I am going to complain to the orderly officer."

It sounded so genuine that he thought it was true until it was explained that these people, like the barber and the dhobi wallah, followed regiments around and attached themselves to them. A lot of them were brought up in the same regiments by their fathers, who did the same job or provided the same service, so they had a very pronounced regional British accent.

Because of the heat, everyone only worked in the Forge in the morning and that was from 6am until 1pm. This was a corrugated tin building and by 9 o'clock it was like being in an oven. In three months Giles was down to 133 pounds (65kg). Then they had the afternoon off until 6pm, when they had an hour's work, usually in the stables or the dog kennels.

So at last to the forge, where Giles was to learn more about farriery and how to do it (the army way). It turned out that there was a vacancy for a Farrier Sergeant in the forge and as there were three candidates, there was to be a contest to see who was best.

All had to shoe a horse, but as the other two were ex-wartime Farriers and Giles was a mere sprog the result was a forgone conclusion especially as one of the examiners was CSM Crisp. Anyway Giles ended up having to shoe under Farrier Sergeant Tam Sutherland, a Scotsman, and Farrier Lance Corporal Morgan, a Welshman (otherwise known as Shoey Morgan).

It wasn't such a bad thing as Tam Sutherland was a very good Farrier who taught Giles a lot, and in fact ended up as a Farrier to the Queen's household. Shoey Morgan on the other hand, had a hell of a lot of experience with mules and as there was a Mule company in the area, he was useful in showing Giles the knack of getting shoes on mules especially their first set, which at times could be very exciting.

On a day-to-day basis, Giles and his colleagues spent their time, purchasing, preparing and breaking mules for army use. The mules were purchased from the Indian or Pakistan army breeding farms, or more latterly from civilian sources in Cyprus. They were used throughout the region – just as Giles had done, when delivering water to the pinned down Leicestershires. Those spare were shipped to Korea and Malaysia for use in the conflicts there.

Life changed for Giles when he was breaking a mule. He was on its back, being thrown around, when the mule swerved and ran under the overhanging roof of the compound. It then bucked, launching him off its back, straight up into the overhanging roof beams, and then back down onto the hard paving slabs. The mule skipped away leaving Giles crumpled on the floor.

"Are you OK?" asked Jim Dobson. "Give me your hand."

But something was wrong. Giles couldn't move.

They put him on a stretcher and took him off to the base hospital where they found that he had broken his back.

He spent the next 12 weeks in plaster and traction, which kept him out of a lot of the skirmishes around the base, but he was kept up to date as either Sam or Jim would come and tell him what was happening.

This is how he learned how Sam and a couple of other dog handlers had cleared a mob gathered around the barracks entrance, spoiling for a fight. A lieutenant had called for armed troops to put the insurrection down using rifles, if necessary, but Sam suggested an alternative strategy.

Muslims consider dogs to be dirty, and are terrified that they may be bitten by such an animal.

Sam put the dogs on long 10-yard-long leads and then let them loose on the crowd. The dogs charged snarling at the mob, who parted, scattered and then vanished. In seconds the street was empty, with no-one hurt and no shots fired.

Jim on the other hand had suffered a loss. There had been a spate of thefts in the camp, and everyone knew it was the indigenous workers who were stealing anything that wasn't nailed down. Jim had lost his watch, which he had put on the side of the sink whilst he shaved. When he looked down, it was gone.

The theft that made everyone laugh, was when four soldiers woke up in the morning, to find that the carpet, that their beds rested on and where they had been sleeping, had been stolen, literally from underneath them.

The guards at the gate searched each worker as he left, and never found anything.

They were being robbed but couldn't seem to do anything about it.

Sam and the dog handlers came to the rescue, leaving the dogs to roam the compound. The dogs were trained to accept orders from the soldiers, but to attack and bite anyone else.

The thefts stopped, when one worker ran past the gate guard and out of the compound with the back of his jellaba torn open, his backside in plain view, with a dog hanging off the tatters of the cloth.

"He won't nick any more watches," said Sam, as he recalled the dog. And he was right.

Moascar was the home for veterinary corps and the remount centre in the area. It was also home for several British regiments, who were used to guard the Suez canal itself and 'police' against the guerrilla activities.

Giles had recovered from his broken back and after a month of rehabilitation, had resumed normal duties.

One evening he was sitting in the mess tent with Sandy eating his dinner. It was common to have catcalls and banter between soldiers from different regiments, but on this occasion the normal banter and comments started to be replaced with louder and angrier shouts.

On one side of the tent was a squad of commandos and on the other were some Scots guards, with Giles and Sandy sitting in no man's land, between them.

"It's goin' to kick off, ba," growled Sandy, who had a fine-tuned antenna for trouble.

He unbuckled and took off his belt, wrapped one end round his left hand and passed the other end to Giles. "Howd this, an' don't let go. We stand back to back an' nobody marn't come up behoind us."

Giles did as he was told, and they stood up. Just as the soldiers on both sides of the tent rose to their feet. The shouting had stopped, and each side looked at the other waiting for someone to make a move.

"Howd yew haard, ba," said Sandy.

A guard stepped forward, and as if by common consent, he had broken an invisible boundary. Soldiers from both sides roared and charged toward each other.

The two tides of bodies swirled past Giles, ignoring him as if he wasn't there. Behind he could hear 'tok' and knew that Sandy was working. 'tok', again. Giles looked over his shoulder and could see Sandy scanning those soldiers nearest him, cocked and ready. When one moved just that little bit too close, 'tok', and he went down to join the pile of bodies on the floor.

Giles was brought back to his own situation when a squaddie punched him on the forehead whilst he wasn't looking. It was a useless punch, but it hurt and Giles swung round, flailing his right arm in front of him. There followed a couple of seconds whilst both looked at each other, waving their arms menacingly, but not actually engaging. Sandy reached over Giles" shoulder, 'tok' and the face was gone.

Now Giles could look around him and survey the chaos.

These were elite fighting men, who had been trained to kill using stilettoes, garottes and bayonets. To gouge their opponent's eyes out and crush their windpipes, but in the heat of the moment, all training had left them and it was replaced with whirling arms just like in a school playground.

To his left, he saw two men, each holding the other's arms, so neither could punch the other. Locked together in a weird waltz, they seemed to be taking it in turns to try and knee their opponent in the balls. Finally the commando, tired with this ball-kicking dance, leaned forward and headbutted his opponent, who collapsed to the floor in a heap of khaki. He turned and Giles could see blood coursing from the bridge of his nose. He wobbled for a second, then his eyes turned up inside his eyelids, and he too slid down to land on top of his opponent.

By this time, Sandy was finding it hard to reach targets because of the bodies stacked around his feet. He pulled Giles 3 yards to their left, and resumed his work. But by now the ferocity had burned out of all but the wildest soldiers, and most stood with their hands on their knees, breathing heavily and bleeding onto the mess room floor.

Sandy stepped over and finished off a couple of soldiers who didn't know when to stop. He came out of his fighter's crouch and unwound the belt from his hand and looked around. Giles heard Sandy counting under his breath.

"Eight," he concluded. "I got eight. Nine if we count your one." Giles would swear that he saw a smile flit across Sandy's lips,

"Let's go afore the MPs get here, ba."

"Yew are goin' on an 'oliday," Crisp informed Giles.

This time, there was no particular danger (at least he assumed so). He was going to patrol the desert Bedouin tribes, checking their livestock for Anthrax and Foot and Mouth.

Animal checking was a common request from the local countries, and they relied upon the Veterinary corps' skills and experience, to provide this service. The British government looked on it as good Public Relations, and the local countries got free medicine and veterinary services.

Basically, Giles had been given three camels, supplies and a Sais (Arab guide). He and the Sais would travel through the deserts, looking for wandering tribesmen, and checking their animals. The tour would last for 3 months.

Given that the Bedouin were nomadic and usually moved their whole tribe every 3-5 days, there was no fixed itinerary. In fact, even armed with maps, Giles wondered exactly how he would manage to do this.

This is where the Sais came in.

Each morning, the Sais would wake up and prepare coffee. Then he would stand up, seemingly sniff the air and announce "This direction. Three days," and sure enough on the third day, having travelled across featureless, blazing desert, not seeing a single living thing, he and the Sais would ride over the crest of a hill or wadi and there would be a Bedouin encampment.

Giles assumed that the Sais knew where the encampment was, but then learned that the tribe had only arrived there on the previous day. So the Sais had known where the tribe would be three days in the future, rather than where it had been when they started.

This happened time and time again. Each time, the Sais would sniff the air and point, and sure enough one, two or three days later, they would come across a new encampment.

And so, Giles and the Sais travelled through the eastern deserts of Egypt, and on to the foot of the newly found Israel.

The Israelis were not very happy about Giles and the Sais, and they were halted at the border.

You have to understand, people make borders, but the Bedouin didn't recognise them. To them, the land was the land and sticking a flag into it didn't make any difference to them.

After a quick radio conversation with their seniors, the border guards allowed them to continue.

And on Giles travelled, through southern Israel, to Jordan, Petra, Wadi Rum and on.

By now Giles was starting to pick up some Arabic. The Sais spoke English, but in a halting, basic way and well there wasn't much else to do but talk, day after day. He turned out to be an excellent student. It would cost more at Berlitz, but you couldn't get more immersive that sitting on a camel week after week.

They had been travelling over a month, when they came across another Bedouin encampment in Wadi Rum.

As before, Giles was introduced and was shown and inspected their animals, and once all was done, they set about treating him as a guest of the highest importance.

This was their tradition, and they would put on a banquet in honour of Giles. Not only for courtesy but also to demonstrate that they weren't poor (even though they were often poor as dirt).

Giles protests were dismissed, and they would kill a small sheep or goat in his honour, even though this was a major part of their wealth. Then a spread would be laid on huge brass plates a yard wide, each containing a mountain of rice and pieces of succulent lamb.

Etiquette demanded that, as the guest, Giles was offered the sheep's eyeballs. This is a tricky situation. As a guest he was being offered a prized delicacy and refusal would certainly cause offence. Luckily, he managed to avoid this by claiming that this was against his religion.

Giles had learned that Arabic is a very flowery language, and conversations were very formal, rather than straightforward.

"I would like to thank you, our guest, for bestowing your exalted presence on us, and providing such service in the care of our animals," said the chief.

"it is my greatest pleasure, to travel across the desert, and to come upon a man of such learning. I thank you for your hospitality," replied Giles.

"Now that we have eaten, can I offer you our humble coffee?" he enquired. "it is a pleasure I have learned to enjoy and a perfect conclusion to our meal. I have never travelled to your lands, but I learn and understand that you English like milk in your coffee,"

"It is true, and I am pleased and surprised to find a man that knows of our customs. I would love milk in my coffee."

Now, in the desert, milk is not common, and the usual source is from a camel, that is milked into a gourd. The gourd previously having been urinated into and emptied. The slight urine traces served to cause the milk to coagulate and form a curd, which the Bedouin use to make a type of cheese.

At this moment, a camel roared and then thundered past the tent, followed a few steps later by an ululating tribeswoman waving a gourd.

There was a pause of a few seconds, and the chief leaned over to Giles and said confidentially, "Milk may be some time."

And so it went, for three months, down into northern Saudi Arabia and then back through Jordan, Israel and Egypt returning to Moascar.

He was exhausted, and after three months of rice, goat and unleavened bread, he had lost quite a bit of weight, which considering he was already slim, made him positively gaunt.

The first thing he did was to walk to the NAAFI, where he bought and ate a whole loaf of white bread, cheddar cheese and pickled onions.

"Holtom reporting, sir," said Giles, as he returned to camp.

"Nice to see you Holtom," said Lieutenant Spurry. "There's a Captain Brown would like a word with you. He's waiting over at the Colonel's office."

And so, Giles had to report to the Men in Grey coats again.

This particular Captain Brown was dressed for the climate, and was wearing a light linen suit.

"Ah, Holtom. Nice to see you again. I understand that you have been spending a little time in Israel. I'd like to ask you a few questions, if you don't mind."

And so, Giles was debriefed about Israel, the sentiment in Jordan about the Israelis, the Arab situation, the location of any soldiers he had seen, etc.

"I understand that you can speak a little of the lingo," said Brown.

"Yes. Sir, a little."

"Keep it up. It could be useful."

Having been away, Giles was rewarded with a week's leave, but everywhere was more than a week away, so mostly he spent his time in cafes around Ismailia and in writing to Elizabeth.

"seein' as though you did so well, I've decided to send you out on another tour," Crisp informed him.

Three more months of riding a camel in burning heat and drinking sour alkali water were not Giles idea of fun, and he murmured, grumbled and carped his way back to the barracks.

Two days later, he was off on his travels again. Just him, three camels, supplies, and a Sais.

The patrol passed in exactly the same way as before, only by the end of it, Giles' command of Arabic had improved considerably and he was able to converse with tribesmen without needing the Sais' translation.

"Holtom reporting, sir," said Giles, as he returned to camp.

"Ah, Holtom. There's another Captain Brown would like a word with you." said Lieutenant Spurry.

This time, at the end of the debriefing, Captain Brown said, "I think it's time you were promoted, don't you? I will have a word with your commanding officer."

And so, Private Holtom became Corporal Holtom.

It was 1953, and Giles had been in the army for 3 years and away from home almost all of this time. He was also given enough leave time for him to return to the UK for a week, where he met up with Elizabeth. He went to visit her and her parents in her home town of Dewsbury Yorkshire.

Rex, her father was a 'man from the Pru', who used to collect insurance premiums and payments from the local housewives on his rounds. Previously, he had worked in the mines as a mining engineer and had been followed there by Elizabeth's brother Colin.

Elizabeth was bowled over by Giles'. Maybe it was his exotic travel and tales of the desert, Ethiopia and such, but in any case, they decided to get married, and this was planned the next time he could get leave.

Giles returned to Melton Mowbray, where he was told that he would not be going back to Egypt. He was now going to be assigned to stay in the UK for a year.

In which case, he asked, "Could I ask for permission to marry?"

"By all means," said the Colonel, "in fact, get it done whilst you are here, and she can go with you to Germany."

It was a choice of do it now or wait for another 18 months when Giles would be back in the UK.

Whilst it was sudden, Giles and Liz had actually known each other for 2 years, and so it didn't seem too rushed. They didn't want to wait. And so, it was set up, arranged and done within a couple of weeks.

The wedding took place on a drizzly, overcast Yorkshire day, with Giles in his formal dress uniform. The only person he had from his side was his friend Ted Simmonds, as his best man.

He was surrounded by the Ganter family, who were dour, strict Presbyterians. They were mostly nonplussed by an Essex farm boy who seemed to have travelled all around the world – or at least out of Yorkshire.

Generally speaking, they considered him in the same way as people looking at a two headed calf in a circus.

And he didn't put cheese on his slice of wedding cake either. A strange lad indeed.

◆ ◆ ◆

After a short 5-day honeymoon in Scarborough, the married couple returned to Melton Mowbray to find that Germany had been postponed and he was to stay in the UK for a few more months.

As Giles was an NCO, he and Liz were given married quarters. These were small, simple, pre-fabricated cabin bungalows, comprising a bedroom, a sitting room, kitchen and bathroom. They had all mod cons, including a gas fire, a gas cooker, and basic furniture. They even had a fridge!

Just for comparison, Giles' parents, Bill and Joan cooked on a paraffin stove. Whereas Liz's parents, Rex and Edie had a meat safe and used the cellar to keep food cool. Both families had outside toilets. In fact, it took about another 10-12 years before Rex bought their first house, for the princely sum of £600!

They were in heaven. Compared to their parent's living conditions, they were really well off.

Not only this, Liz was now part of a group – soldier's wives. A couple were sergeant's but the majority were officer's wives.

The klatch was run with a very strict hierarchy, and Liz as a corporal's wife was at the bottom, with the Colonel's wife at the top.

"Oh, you worked before," said one wife, "How interesting. You must tell me all about it, some time." She had never worked in her life.

Liz had trained and was qualified as a State Registered Nurse (SRN) in the newly created National Health Service. The work had been arduous with long shifts.

In those days antibiotics were still very new and they still used things like sulphur powder to dress wounds, and hospital wards were cleaned out with concentrated bleach every day. In fact hospitals all smelled like bleach until around the mid 60's when they started using different cleaning agents.

Now, she was a serviceman's wife, and it was expected that she wouldn't work, except maybe to do things for charity and the WI. So what was she to do?

Well in the early 50's, every woman had a sewing machine, and they made their own and their children's clothes. Well Liz was young, slim and good looking, and now she had a chance to make herself some clothes that made her look like Grace Kelly. All she needed was the patterns and some cloth. This worked very well, because Liz had the necessary skills, and now she had the time.

Pretty soon she had a couple of cocktail dresses, and she could attend parties with the other wives.

"You know, your accent is quite, quite charming," said the colonel's wife, "although when you arrived, I must admit, I didn't understand everything you said. Ha ha."

Liz's broad Yorkshire accent soon disappeared, to be replaced by home counties.

Yes. She had started as a mining engineer's daughter from Yorkshire drinking bitter shandies, and now she had her own fridge and was drinking Manhattans. Not only did she have a house with all mod-cons, she had made a large step up the social ladder as well.

They had been married for three months, and Liz confirmed that she was pregnant. They were going to have a child.

Up to this time, Giles had mostly concentrated on working with Horses, and now the army decided (as he was a 'rabies expert') that he should become a dog expert as well.

This not only involved normal veterinary medicine and surgery, but also dog handling and training.

The army didn't train dogs for obedience, or looks. They trained them to kill. The dogs were either used as compound guard dogs or in combat. In some particular circumstances, digs were given specialised training, for example to sniff out soldiers hiding in tunnels underground, or even to detect explosives, and Giles learned all of these techniques.

Basic attack dog training is quite straightforward.

Step 1. All you needed to do was to be able to encourage a dog to attack on command. Often as not this simply entailed shouting "attack, attack," excitedly whilst pointing the dog at a target. The dogs soon got the idea, and joined in enthusiastically.

Of course for this you needed a target, and as Giles was now a Corporal, he could avail himself of a private, attack, for the use of.

The unhappy private was initially given a complete body suit, heavily padded all over, as you didn't know where the dog would bite them.

Dogs love to chase, so the easiest start to training was to give the unhappy private a 25-yard start, and then shout "attack." The dog's natural instinct was to chase the baddie and off they went.

Now you had the problem of calling off the dog, and sometimes this was not so easy. Some dogs simply refused to stop and had to be dragged off their victims – and in some cases turning on their handlers.

These were not good dogs.

The other point about this was to imprint a command word to get them to release. This had to be special and hard to guess, for example banana. Otherwise the baddies would simply shout "release," and the dog would stop. The baddies would never guess banana.

So, now, prepared with their new command words, the dogs could be directed at someone, attack them and then called off.

It was time to test this, and so the private was suited up again with help from Giles and his friend Ted Simmonds. This time he would be set to stand a 100 yards away, so that they could test that the dog could be directed over a distance.

"OK, go," Giles shouted and the heavy suited private lolloped and lumbered off over the field.

"Attack," he said, pointing out the target, and the dog shot off like a bullet, racing across the ground.

The private had got to the edge of the field, which was bounded by a small stream. He stopped and turned round, just as the dog launched itself through the air and planted its paws on his chest. He shot backwards down the bank and disappeared from view.

Giles and Ted ambled over to the stream bank where the dog was patiently watching the private, who was at the bottom of the stream.

The suit weighed up to 100lbs (50kg) and now that it was filled with water, the poor private had sunk to the bottom and was pinned there.

Looking at the poor man, staring up at them from under 3 feet of water was the funniest thing that they had ever seen, and they collapsed laughing on the bank. It took quite a while before it occurred to them, that maybe to private was drowning and that he couldn't get up because of the weight of the waterlogged suit.

They both jumped in and fished him, coughing, out onto the bank.

"Banana," said Giles, belatedly, to the dog.

Step 2. Now that the dog can be directed to attack and can be recalled, they need to be trained to attack specific parts of the body.

It is no good if a dog attacks a baddie's leg, as the baddie can simply shoot the dog.

They have to be taught to go for the throat, but only after they have disarmed an opponent.

So now the dogs were trained with privates wearing arm and throat protection. First, they would go for the gun hand, biting until the gun is dropped, and then switching to the throat.

They had a selection of dogs to train. Some were good, obedient and biddable, whereas some were just vicious. The army was happy with both types, but the vicious dogs could often only be controlled by one, single handler.

One such dog was Caesar, seemingly a cross between a mastiff and a donkey. He was a dog that would attack but could not be recalled. The dog handlers would push a broom handle through the wires of the kennel and under Caesar's collar, pinning him in place. Then one brave person would open the kennel and put his food inside, hoping that the dog would go for the food, rather than the handler.

Everyone hoped that, once trained, Caesar would be given to someone else.

"If I ever get given that dog, I'll shoot it," said Wally Manton.

As luck would have it, Giles was given some leave, when the dogs were assigned, and he and Liz spent a few days in Essex with his family.

On his return, he learned that Wally Manton had indeed been given Caesar, but he was now in hospital.

Giles went down to visit him, to see what had happened.

"The bloody dog attacked me," said Wally.

"I thought you said you would shoot it."

"I tried. But every time I reached for my gun it bit my arm, and when I stopped, it bit me in the throat. They pulled him off me in less than 30 seconds."

Wally had 149 puncture wounds.

Along with the basic attack skills, the dogs also needed to be trained to be obedient and controllable.

In the end, proper Army dogs are some of the most highly trained and effective, obedient animals it is possible to find.

Whilst Giles, learned all of the necessary skills, he never used them very much, until later in his career, as we shall see. However, his friends, Ted Simmonds and Sam Perrie went on to specialise in this area. Sam ending up as a celebrity dog trainer who was responsible for defining and writing the current police dog training manual.

Liz was 5 months into her term when she miscarried. It was a little girl. She was distraught.

Giles had always wanted a daughter. He also took things badly, as, but he wasn't much help or use.

Things were different in those days, and women were expected to 'get over it'. The only help they had, if any, came from their family.

Liz was very lucky. Whilst she didn't have her family around, she was part of the army wives' klatch, and they rallied around, helped her and provided support.

It was the end of 1954, and Giles was now both a horse and dog specialist. He had been in Melton Mowbray for a year, without any problems. CSM Crisp was still stuck out in Egypt, and out of Giles life.

They now posted him to Germany.

Meanwhile in the news:

Правда
Soviet Soldiers taught secret code to disarm British Army dogs.
The information ministry has informed us that a banana is a capitalist fruit like our potato but not as tasty.

12.   GERMANY

As Liz was going with him, Giles decided to drive to Germany, and he needed a car.

These are easy to pick up at any army base, as someone is always being posted elsewhere. It is a common occurrence for someone to walk into the barracks or canteen and announce, "anyone want a car? I'm off to Korea/Malaya/Hong Kong/Egypt."

Giles got himself a nice American Lincoln. It was almost 20 years old, and looked like Al Capone's getaway car, but it had a huge engine and went like stink. Petrol was cheap in those days, and so 10mpg didn't bother him much.

And so, with all their belongings packed, Giles and Liz took the ferry from Harwich, and then through Holland and into Germany. For Liz, this was the first time she had ever been abroad.

They were going to Paderborn, which is a medium sized town in Westphalia. This was to the East of the cities of the Ruhr and was the British sector of the front against Russia and the East Germans. The American sector was further south. It was mostly forested countryside and hills, filled with half-timbered houses in quaint mediaeval villages.

Giles drove, whilst Liz navigated, using a map that he had managed to get hold of. At each intersection and roundabout, Liz would direct, "Follow the sign to Münster." or, "take the 476."

She giggled, as he explained to her that 'ausfahrt' meant exit. It was the first German word she had learnt.

After a while, she asked, "When do we get to this place, Umleitung? It's signed on every roundabout."

After Giles had stopped laughing, this is when Liz learned that 'Umleitung' means diversion. It was her second German word.

The married accommodation was in some ways, even better than Melton Mowbray. Liz marvelled at the secondary glazing which she had never seen before. She immediately recognised its value in the freezing, snowy German winter.

Apart from this, everything was almost the same as the UK. She had access to all British goods she wanted in the NAAFI, and was again welcomed into the local army wives' klatch.

When spring came, a little man knocked at her door, and as she answered, he doffed his cap and walked past her and through to the back garden, where he cut the grass with a scythe. She even had her own gardener.

Giles was not the only new soldier that had been posted to Paderborn. The commanding officer was also being replaced by his old friend Lieutenant (now Captain) John Spurry.

This was good news for Giles, as Spurry had always been a fair and supportive officer. He had known about CSM Crisp's animosity to Giles, and in his own way, had tried to curb the excesses.

"You need to be able to control your emotions," Spurry once advised Giles. "If you don't like something, you need to be able to keep that from showing on your face. As it is, your thoughts stick out like dog's balls and someone, like an CSM, can take advantage, making you do things you don't want to do, or by denying you those things that you want."

"You won't get very far in the army, if you can't keep your face still and emotionless, as required."

"Still, I would love to play poker against you. I think I would win a lot of money."

◆ ◆ ◆

This transfer did present Spurry with a problem. It all started at the formal handover of the command.

Basically, this entailed all of the command being paraded, inspected and then handed over by the old captain to the new one. This would then be formally documented and signed, and the old captain could then leave for his next assignment.

"20," said Captain Spurry, "I counted 20 men."

"That's right," said Captain Maclear.

"But this inventory states that the command consists of 21 men."

"Look old boy, don't rock the boat. There were 20 men here when I arrived and signed for them, even though the documentation says 21. If you complain, then there will be an investigation, and neither of us would want that. Don't worry. He's somewhere and he'll turn up eventually. He's still drawing his pay. We just don't know where."

So, John Spurry signed.

◆ ◆ ◆

The first job Giles had to do was attend to a pet collie owned by the wife of a Colonel that was also sited on the base.

Apparently, it had fallen into some form of stupor. It was living and breathing, but otherwise unresponsive and cataleptic.

Giles brought it into the surgery to have a look. He decided that he needed to x-ray it, and he and his assistant prepared things. The dog was laid on a table and the apparatus set up. The lights were dimmed, and both went to stand behind the lead screen.

What neither had noticed was that a bottle of ether had been knocked over by one of them, and the liquid had evaporated into gas and was leaking out. Luckily ether is heavier than air, so it just covered the floor.

Unfortunately, ether is also highly flammable, and when they went to switch on some equipment, it must have produced a spark at floor level which caused the ether to explode.

Being inside an explosion is obviously very disorientating, and it took several seconds before Giles managed to think straight again. He looked around.

The blast had been contained by the curtains, so the windows were intact, and the only damage seemed to have been to the light bulbs which had shattered.

Giles looked around for the dog, only to find that it wasn't there. A check unearthed a few singed hairs but otherwise, showed that it was no longer in the room and had disappeared.

"Bloody hell," thought Giles, "I've blown up the Colonel's dog."

This was not going to end well.

Giles put on a clean uniform and marched over to the Colonel's quarters to apologise, where he met his wife.

"Ah, corporal. So nice to see you. I don't know what you did, but Trixie is as good as new," she said, indicating the collie, who was tucking into some food.

"No problem, ma'am," he replied, patting the dog and feeling the slightly singed coat under his fingers.

Whatever the problem had been, the explosion had resurrected the dog and it had run home.

◆ ◆ ◆

In the spring, Liz announced that she was pregnant again.

This was wonderful news for both of them, except that Giles had been called to Captain Spurry's office to be told that he had been proposed to go to the Army language training school. The recommendation had come from a Captain Brown.

"It will mean six months away, and then you might get reposted, depending upon where they need your skills," Said Capt. Spurry. "Of course, you will probably get a promotion and pay rise as well."

After discussion with Liz, it seemed that the promotion and money were important, and that Liz would be perfectly happy living in her little house with the NAAFI nearby and her own gardener, so Giles accepted and off he went.

This part of the story was told to me, once, by Liz. Giles never discussed it, and it wasn't part of his repertoire of anecdotes.

My understanding was that, this was basic spy school. He would learn a language to a level where he could blend in as a local, or some such.

"What language?" I asked.

"He never said, but the only people we were afraid of at that time were the Russians," said Liz.

Anyway, he was sent to a specialist training school, probably Beaconsfield in Buckinghamshire. The approach was total immersion, and on arrival, all students were given basic phrases to learn in their target language. Things like, "What is this?" and "how do you say... ?", and then they were thrown into the deep end to learn.

All conversation was in the language, and they were penalised if they used English. The idea was for them to learn like children, to think and talk in the language as second nature.

Some of their life was run from announcements on a tannoy.

"Обед сейчас подается," the tannoy squawked, and some of the students got up and left. Those who hadn't understood the announcement, sat there, and missed lunch (which is what the announcement had said). They learned pretty quickly - or went hungry.

The army had decided that all information both in and out of the camp was to be minimal and all letters censored. So Giles' letters arrived at Liz saying, "I am ████████████████████████████████. All is ████████████. Here we ███████████████████████████ but ████████████████████████████████████, OK. Love, Giles"

And Liz's response was "Darling, the baby is doing really well and I ha had no problems with my preganancy, and ████████████. ████████████ NAAFI, ████████████████████████. We ████████, and ████████████, but not ████████████. Love Liz."

By all accounts, Giles was very adept, and was picking up the language well. The only problem he had was the lack of communication with the outside world. Specifically, the absence of any news about Liz and the baby was driving him nuts.

He didn't want to miss the birth of his child, and, after her miscarriage, he was worried that Liz might not be OK. Of course, he had no way of telling what the situation really was, as all information was being censored. This became such a concern, that after 4 months, he failed himself out of the course, and returned back to his unit.

So, no sergeant's stripes and no spying for Giles.

Moving forward in time, to just 2 years before his death, I was sitting across from Giles drinking white wine in the small hours of the morning, when I asked him, "what about the time you went to the army language school to become a Russian spy?"

"What?" said Giles, "Who told you that?"

"Mum. She said you were sent away just before I was born, to learn Russian."

"Rubbish," he said. "I was sent to learn Arabic. As I had a good grounding, and had impressed the locals, the 'men in grey coats' decided that I would be a good asset for British interests in Arabia. Most likely Persia (nowadays Iran), as Britain and the US were vying for their oil, and they wanted to place advisors into the area, that were accepted, understood and trusted by the locals."

So Giles wasn't going to be a Russian Spy. He was intended to be a British (Foreign Office) asset trying to get BP into Persia, and in the end he became neither.

Although in another instance, when I was a teenager, I do remember him being accosted by a carpet seller on the promenade in Beziers in the South of France. Giles didn't speak French, and so responded in German. The vendor didn't understand German, and tried Spanish and Italian, to no avail. They then both settled on Arabic, and spent 10 minutes happily haggling over a carpet.

"You didn't buy it then," I said.

"Oh, no. But he was just happy to be able to get through to me, and we had a good chat."

It was the only time I heard him speak Arabic.

◆ ◆ ◆

Back in Paderborn, Giles found that Liz was now 7 months gone and was perfectly fine and glowing – apart from her strange cravings. She had mad desires for Dunkel Bier (a weak, German dark beer) and Giles was frequently sent out of the camp at 2am to drive to the local Gasthaus, knock up the proprietor, and buy a bottle of beer. After the second time, the landlord gave Giles a case of the beer and told him not to come back.

And so, on October 6th 1955, we come to the most important part of the story. I, Mark David Holtom, was born.

This happened in the Army hospital in Rinteln, a small town, just down the road from Hamelin (yes, where the rats come from).

Being an Army hospital, it was geared up for male patients and to cater for the army's particular injuries and ailments (which were mostly venereal). This meant that Liz had her own private room, and dedicated doctor and nurse. It was just like going private.

In those days the husband was not allowed or expected, to attend the birth, so Giles turned up later.

"They've just rung. You've got yourself a little boy. Cut away now, Jolly," he was told by Capt. Spurry.

He turned up at Liz's room to find her in tears.

"He's deformed," she wailed.

It seems that, during the birth, my nose had become dislodged and bent, and it was now occupying some territory under my left eye, pointing to my ear.

"Look at him. He's so ugly." Apparently, I had a face that not even a mother could love.

Giles picked me up, looked at me, gave a start and then forced a smile onto his face.

"That's only temporary," he assured her, as he hurriedly put me back in the cot.

He then left to go and wet the baby's head with the boys. After looking at me, he needed a drink

In case Giles was posted away, leaving Liz with a brand-new baby, he arranged for her to have a dog for company and protection. She didn't need it, but felt better for it being there, and so, he brought home Saba, an Irish Red Setter. It seems that Saba was a bit of a nervous dog, when alone, so Giles also brought along Astra, an Alsatian, so they were company for each other. Liz's first two dogs were British army trained war dogs.

"You are wanted by the Russians," said Captain Spurry. "Actually, they have an outbreak of Rabies in East Berlin, and they have asked the British army for help. They think that the person we send over will probably be a spy, so they have asked us to send the 'expert' that we used in Crete, which was, er, you. So you are off the East Berlin."

It was the end of 1955, and 6 years before the Berlin wall was built, although there was a lot of barbed wire. Berlin was split into 4 jurisdictions (US, English, French and Russian), just as Vienna was. This time there was no international sector and no fraternisation between the East and West, except at certain crossing points, like Checkpoint Charlie.

The former allies did share one common task, which was to guard 7 Nazi war criminals in Spandau prison, which was situated in the British sector. Each country would assume the responsibility of guarding the prison for a month, on a rotating basis. The Russians, then the Americans, etc. As before, the Russians would install bugs for the Americans, who would strip the place to find, and then replace them with bugs of their own. The French and British would do the same.

And so, within a couple of days, Giles found himself on a train carrying about 100 troops bound for West Berlin to garrison Spandau.

West Berlin was completely surrounded and enclosed within East Germany, and any train or car bound for West Berlin had to travel through the East, and its associated checkpoints, and it was at the last one of these, on the border with West Berlin, where the train was stopped by Russian border guards. This was a normal occurrence, and happened for every single troop train going into and out of West Berlin.

The Captain in charge ordered that all blinds to be drawn down, so that the Russians couldn't see into the carriage. He went to the window and stuck his head out.

"What seems to be the problem, old son?" asked the Captain, knowing full well what the problem was.

"How many soldiers on train?" asked a Russian Kapitan from the platform.

"Sorry, old boy, but you don't have the right or authority. We are the replacement garrison for Spandau, which comes here every 3 months, as you know."

The Russian shouted an order and his troops lined up on the platform, facing the train carriages.

In response, the Captain issued orders for his men to stand ready within the train.

"You don't go until I see soldiers," said the Russian.

"Sorry, old boy, but I'm not letting you," replied the Captain.

In this escalation, the Kapitan then ordered his men to point their rifles into the carriages, and the British captain ordered his men to do likewise.

This is when Giles sat down on the floor behind the Captain. He looked down the carriage to see the ridiculous sight of about 25 soldiers pointing their rifles at the carriage curtains, not being able to see through them. Along the platform he could see a similar number of Russian troops aiming blindly into the train.

Giles wanted to laugh. He recognised that this was hysteria, but it didn't stop the fact and he had to stifle himself. He couldn't help seeing the ridiculousness of a situation where 50 soldiers were pointing guns at each other, without being able to see their targets. They were expected to shoot at a curtain and hope that they hit someone, and not be hit themselves. It was just like a children's game of battleships, both laughable – and scary.

With such an impasse, both captains looked at each other though the carriage window. Everyone held their breath.

This could soon go very wrong thought Giles, and I could be shot by mistake.

The Russian Kapitan put his head through the window and into the train, trying to look along the carriage. At which the British Captain smartly pulled up the glass, hitting the Russian under the jaw before he pulled his head back through the frame.

For another couple of seconds nothing happened, as Giles watched the Russian Kapitan, wondering how he would react.

"Tell the driver to move off would you, Sergeant," said the Captain, and after a few seconds the train moved off through the border to West Berlin.

"Happens every bloody time," he said to Giles, as he helped him to his feet from off the floor.

Once in West Berlin, Giles was then formally taken to Checkpoint Charlie and handed over to the Russians. And so, began the East Berlin Rabies clearance.

The Russians suspected Giles might be a spy. After all, wouldn't they send a spy in the same circumstances? True, but if he was a spy, he wouldn't understand Rabies, would get bitten and die. If he was an expert, he would know what to do, survive, and show that he wasn't a spy.

But just in case, make sure he doesn't see anything.

And so Giles was billeted in with a Russian platoon, in some local barracks. Here he came across all of the things which we now associate with Russia; black bread, vodka and caviar. To be honest, he preferred white bread, whisky and he thought their jam was off, but he didn't like to be impolite.

One day, he woke up and looked out of his billet to see the whole company paraded on the square outside. They were being issued winter uniforms.

Each soldier was given a heavy, grey greatcoat. They were similar to his own, expect that they were made of thick felt which was much warmer and quite waterproof.

He laughed when he saw that every great coat was the same XXL size. Given that the soldiers ranged from 5'6" to 6'6" (165-195cm), they only fitted the tallest soldiers, and even then, they were quite long. But the shortest soldiers looked like dopey from Snow White, with their coats draped onto the ground, around their feet.

He stopped laughing when she saw two men come out of the barracks. One had what looked like a wheel on a pole, used to measure distances. On closer inspection, he saw that the wheel had a pointer on the side, tipped with chalk, and the first man used it to walk around a soldier, marking his greatcoat at exactly 6" above the ground. The second man, followed behind and, using these chalk marks, cut the coat to length with a large pair of shears. The offcuts were put into a wheelbarrow, where they could be recycled into more coats.

After just half an hour, each soldier's coat was exactly 6" off the floor, regardless of their height, and the previously comic and slovenly parade now looked very smart and uniform.

The only other incident of note occurred, when a Scottish soldier had been allowed to enter East Berlin and go to the barracks to deliver Giles' pay packet. The guard at the entrance was not letting some British (I'm no British. I'm Scottish) soldier in, and by the same token, Jock (for that was his name) was not about to let some thieving Russian get his hands on a mate's pay packet.

When Giles heard the shouting and swearing in English, he went to investigate the problem. He arrived at the barracks gate to find a (slightly drunk) Scotsman screaming abuse at a (probably equally drunk) Soviet returning the abuse in Russian. This debate was rapidly escalating into an international incident.

However, as soon as Giles received his pay packet, normal fraternal relations were resumed, and Jock was prevailed upon to try a vodka or two before he left.

It should be noted, for clarity that all Scots in the corps were called Jock, except Jock, because that was his actual name, so he was called 'Mac'. In the same way, all Welsh were called Taffy. And if your surname was White or Gates your nicknames were pre-ordained to be Chalky and Pearly. The army has very little imagination.

Giles instructed the Russians as to how to conduct the rabies clearance, and was given a troop of soldiers to help him. As before, they would round up and corner the dogs and secure them with a noose on the end of a pole, where he would euthanize them. The actual clearance worked better than it had in Crete, in that he didn't get bitten, and the vaccine stayed in the duck's eggs instead of his gut.

In the evening, Giles was taken back to the barracks, and lived, ate and drank with his (new) comrades. Given that they didn't speak English and he had no Russian, conversation was by nature cursory, but a good time, and a lot of drink, was had by all.

A fortnight later, Giles had finished his stint, and cleaned up East Berlin of Rabies. Armed with a couple of bottles of vodka, he returned to West Berlin, where he met, as you might imagine, a couple of Captains Brown wearing grey coats.

One day, back at camp, a new face appeared. It was Private Nobbs, and he made his way to the quartermaster's stores.

"Requisition for a new cap band," said Nobbs.

"Why didn't they give you one when you transferred here?" asked the quartermaster.

"They did. That was three years ago."

"I've never seen you. You'd better come with me."

And so, very quickly, private Nobbs found himself before Captain Spurry.

"So, you've been here three years, and nobody has seen you before."

"Yessir."

"But, that's not.., just a minute. You're number bloody 21," exclaimed Spurry triumphantly.

And so, number 21 was found (for it was he), and Nobby Nobbs told his story.

Apparently, he had been sent up into the hills, to a tiny village, we shall call Bad Tothebone, to look after three horses belonging to the army. The sergeant, who had sent him there, was looking for a place to move the horses to, when he was transferred out to Egypt, and Private Nobbs was forgotten, left to fend for himself, until he received further orders – or had worn out his cap band.

He had fed, watered and exercised the horses daily. But after 3 months of receiving no orders, he had relaxed into the local, village life, using the horses to help the locals to cart goods, and plough fields. He had lots of spare time, which he put to good use by learning some German and courting the mayor's daughter.

By the time he had come back down to Paderborn, he was renting the horses out to the farmers to do work, and had a German wife and child.

"Bloody hell," thought John Spurry, after learning all of this. "I hope he didn't call the kid Helmut, or Willie."

"Go with the sergeant," he said. "He will sort you out." And Private Nobbs was taken and installed in the last, empty bed in the barracks.

Giles had been out with the boys, drinking at the local Gasthaus. It was late and they were all walking home in the dark, with just the occasional glow from a cigarette end to be seen.

The walk back to the front gate was about 2km, and one bright spark said, "Why don't we cut across the back field? There's only that little stream to cross, and it isn't deep."

To the drunken committee, this seemed like an excellent idea, as it would save at least 1.5km of walking.

Of course, a bunch of drunk soldiers, crossing a stream is the perfect set-up for any comedy routine, and it didn't fail.

Somehow, the water, that was less than 12 inches deep during the day, had become 3 foot deep at night, and the gently shelving bank had become steep and covered in nettles.

The ford across the stream was about 2 yards wide, and those who managed to find it looked down on their colleagues to their side, who were up to their waists, and in some cases falling head first and disappearing under the surface.

"You know, you can drown in 12 inches of water," said some wag, to a heavily bedraggled friend.

"Fuck off!"

In amongst the noisy and wet debate, Plum Penrose saw a hat floating downstream toward him.

"Who had been wearing a hat?" thought plum. "Ted Simmons."

You need to know that Plum hated Ted Simmons, and so he picked the hat out of the water and proceeded to twist, wring and deform it at much as he could.

Finally, when what he held looked more like a blancmange than a hat, he said, innocently, "Hey Simmons, your hat was floating down the stream. I've got it here."

"It's not mine. I'm wearing my hat," replied Ted.

It was at this point that Plum remembered, he was the only other person wearing a hat that evening.

"Balls."

By the start of 1957, Giles and Liz had been in Germany for two years. He was called to the CO's office.

"You are being transferred to Malaysia. They are looking for dog handlers and trainers in the current fight against the local communists," said Captain Spurry. "You'll be based in Singapore, so it will be a nice place for Liz to live. A good life out there, I understand."

"Oh, by the way, thanks have come back from the Russians for your work with them. You've been promoted to sergeant."

Meanwhile in the news:

Halstead Gazette

Giles Holtom has a son. "We expect him to look more normal when he gets older."

After trip to Berlin, Giles reports, "Russians drink whisky, made from potatoes."

In other news: Potatoes sold out in Halstead area.

Daily Mail

British Army helps out beleaguered Russians' rabies problem in East Berlin.

Правда

Russian Army explains how to eradicate the Capitalist disease, rabies to invited British soldier.

Rabies has been eradicated from all Communist countries, but is endemic in Western Capitalist culture.

DPRK NEWS

Russian Embassy makes gift of
1,000 fresh dogs to the Democratic
People's Republic of Korea.

Our glorious leader, Kim-il Sung was reported
to have said, "Poodle. My favourite."

13.   THE ROAD TO SINGAPORE

Sergeant Giles Holtom was flown to Singapore on military transport via Teheran and Delhi, whilst Liz and the baby went there by steamer and arrived 3 weeks later.

On arrival, Liz found that, as a Sergeant, Giles was allowed to live 'off base' and they had been given a separate army bungalow on top of a hill, overlooking Singapore. Being high up meant that it was only 89% humidity compared to the 90% humidity of the city below.

With such heat and humidity it was that it was impossible to live with the windows closed, and they were left open in every room, to encourage a meagre through flow of damp air. To prevent burglars from just climbing in, each window had iron bars over it, but this didn't help much as they simply used plastic fishing rods to try and 'fish out' your valuables.

Malaya was going through massive changes at this time. There was a low-level police action being fought between the British land owners and the Malaysian Communists that had been going on for nearly 10 years. It was called a 'police action' or an 'emergency' rather than a war simply because the British landowner's possessions and interests would not be covered by insurance (from Lloyds of London) in the event of 'war'.

The war (sorry - police action), was basically a war for independence (supported by many), and the intention of creating a socialist society (supported by the Communists, but few others). This was complicated by the fact that Malay society was heavily factionalised. Consisting of indigenous Malays, Chinese and Indians, all forming their own separate groups, cultures and societies, with little interaction between them.

The communists were predominantly of Chinese background, and the British exploited this by supporting the indigenous Malay faction. Latterly, the British approach to the conflict had been one of 'hearts and minds' and the Malays in return, often provided intelligence and support to British troops.

Within a few months of Giles arriving, Malaya would become an independent country, away from British rule.

The army was based in Changi, which is now Singapore airport, but at that time had been a former Japanese prisoner of war camp taken over by the British.

It was into this situation that he was posted, with the remit to provide, train and look after dogs, used not only for security but also in finding and flushing out communist rebel fighters hidden in the jungle.

"Well if it ain't the fuckin' country boy," said an unwelcome voice, on Giles' arrival at the base. "We don't want you stuck on the base, do we? You want to be out in the Jungle, searching for fuckin' commies, don't you?"

There were few things worse than jungle patrol. it was boring, hot, wet, humid and immensely uncomfortable – and these were the good points. The rest was avoiding poisonous snakes, insects, fever, malaria, and being shot at by communists.

"Don't forget your quinine," laughed Crisp.

So Giles was set up to go on jungle patrols to find communist insurgents but Liz was afraid of being left on her own in the bungalow with open windows.

"Don't worry. I'll fix this," said Giles, and he returned the next day with a long-haired Alsatian war dog called Demon. "Nobody's going to try and burgle you with this dog in the house."

Amazingly, Demon was both calm and gentle with Liz and me, allowing her to get on with things, whilst he babysat me and prevented me from disappearing into the garden – which was potentially filled with snakes.

Life soon settled into a routine, with Giles going on patrol for a couple of weeks and then back to base for a week of down time.

Being a Briton in Singapore, even on a sergeant's salary, afforded a very good standard of living, and pretty soon Giles and Liz were members of the Singapore yacht club and had a 5-metre dinghy to sail to any one of the beaches or islands dotting the sea nearby.

The Dunkel biers of Paderborn were replaced with Singapore slings and Mai Tais.

Giles could afford handmade shirts and Liz had her own silk cocktail dresses for drinks at Raffles afterwards.

At the end of 1957, she would need some new dresses, as Liz found that she was pregnant again. Hopefully, this would be the girl that they both wanted.

Giles had been good at taking his Larium and quinine, but he still caught Malaria and was put into the camp hospital with a raging fever and delirium for over a week.

"Everyone that goes into the jungle swamps gets it," Liz was told. "He will get better in a few days, but will probably suffer from recurring bouts throughout his life."

He did, and later, as a child, it was a strange thing to see Giles suffer from malarial fever in the middle of a Yorkshire winter. Try explaining that to your GP.

Life in the barracks was sometimes a bit strange. Giles was lucky because he lived off base, but he still was confronted with weird problems.

One part of the camp was considered haunted. It was a part of the camp that was previously used to house British PoWs by the Japanese, and people said that this is where many soldiers were tortured and had died.

The local Malay workers said that there were ghosts there and refused to go there at night. They said that you could hear strange howling and screams coming from this area – but then, this was bordered by jungle, so the strange noises could have been coming from there.

Interestingly, whatever Giles felt about this, he found that his dogs refused to go over to this area, changing from assertive and aggressive war dogs to whining curs whenever they were taken close by.

Of coursed being in Singapore, you expect to see exotic animals, but his platoon was less than happy to see a giant monitor lizard walking through the middle of the barrack room. It was about 5 foot long. The soldiers in there at the time, scrambled to climb onto the top of lockers and upper bunks, as the strange visitor hissed his way down the middle of the room, his claws clicking on the tiled floors.

"They're not poisonous – are they?" asked one soldier.

"I'm not sitting here to find out," was the reply.

"Well bloody move it then."

"You move it. I'm not getting down from this locker."

Out on the street, or even in the bungalow's garden, the main problem was snakes. There seemed to be hundreds of varieties of varying sizes, the only common denominator was that they all killed you.

The worst was called the krait, or bootlace snake. It was dangerous, even as a baby, about 9-12 inches long and thinner than your little finger. Basically a glorified worm, except that its bite was extremely poisonous (the 3rd most toxic in the world).

At the time, there was a scare because they had been found to nest up in the trees growing alongside the wide Singapore boulevards, and in the evenings, they frequently dropped out of the trees, landing upon pedestrians walking below.

The King Cobras that were found sometimes were bigger and more poisonous but you could see them from afar and give them a wide berth.

Still, this was all in the city. It was much worse out in the countryside, and worst of all in the jungle swamps. Just where Giles was patrolling.

At least he could get away from it all, sailing with his boat. He had invested in flippers, a facemask and snorkel, before they told him about sea snakes. Christ, the snakes were even chasing you out to sea.

And what about lion fish? Apparently, a scratch from one of its many spines was enough to paralyse you. You might not even get back into the boat.

Shit. Was nowhere safe in this bloody country?

It was time for my brother, Van, to be born and on July 4th 1958 he duly made an appearance.

This time his nose, and even his whole face was fine, except for the colour. He was blue.

"What's wrong with him?" wailed Liz, thinking, "not another one."

"The umbilical cord was caught round his throat. He is a blue baby, but this doesn't last long, and he will be fine," she was assured, and she was right. Within minutes, Van changed from being a midget smurf to looking like Winston Churchill. In other words, a perfectly normal baby.

The expat community was quite small and very privileged, and merely by being in the army and white, was enough to allow entry for Giles and Liz.

The community consisted of rich landowners, playboy aristocracy's 2nd sons (sent to look after their family's plantations), senior and junior officers from all services, embassy staff, and some, very carefully selected local luminaries (his father owns the teak business around KL and he went to Eton).

In the UK, such a disparate group of people would never have been found together, but the alternative of actually mixing with the local populace never really occurred to them, except when they wanted new clothes made.

Interestingly, this was one area where CSM Crisp was not involved in Giles' life. He was just a lowly sergeant (as was Giles), but more importantly, he was not married, and didn't have a pretty wife, who could get him access via the 'wives club'. This meant Giles was invited to parties and Crisp was left to his own devices in the Sergeant's mess.

It was common for Liz and Giles to mix with local plantation owners and millionaires as well as other officers. There was a hierarchy involved, just as there had been with the army wives' klatch in Melton Mowbray. Being a Sergeant, Giles was at the bottom. But even the bottom was a very big step up from anywhere else outside the group.

They received invitations to lots of cocktail parties at select private residences, and even to the British embassy – well it was Malaya's independence celebrations.

They arrived at the British Embassy, dressed in their best and smartest clothes. Giles had to wear a dinner suit, but was expected to have ribbons outlining his campaigns and awards pinned onto his chest. These were a discrete and small set of ribbons, rather than the big gongs, used on parades.

"Holtom?" enquired a uniformed usher, looking at Giles' gold embossed invitation. "Are you related to Mr Holtom in the embassy?"

"No, sir. My family were farmers, not foreign office."

"Well, look him out. You may find you have some connection in common."

And so, Giles wandered into the gathering, moving from one reception room to another, drink in hand, when he looked across the room and saw his uncle Phil.

It is about now, that I have to tell you something from the past.

In the mid 30's, when Giles was just a boy he had an uncle Philip, his father's brother. One day, Philip went out of the house to walk down to the shop to buy a packet of woodbines, and never came back.

When he hadn't returned on the first night, the family thought that he had got drunk somewhere, and on the second night, they assumed that there was a woman involved. But on the third day, and no uncle Phil, they notified the police, and a search was made. They looked in pubs and ditches, and found nothing. He had simply disappeared off the face of the earth.

Six months later, they received a card, postmarked Shanghai, saying that he was fine, but leaving no contact details. What had happened? Nobody knew, and uncle Phil passed into family legend.

Until that evening in 1957, when Giles walked into a reception room in the British Embassy.

"Excuse me, but are you Philip Holtom, the brother of Bill Holtom in Halstead?" enquired Giles.

"I am, yes. How would you know that?" asked a surprised Philip.

"I'm Giles, Bill's son."

Philip didn't recognise Giles, given that he was now 26 and had last seen him over 20 years previously, but once introduced, they retired to a couple of chairs in the corner of the library, to drink a whisky, smoke, and catch up.

Philip's story:

After buying his cigarettes, Philip walked out of the shop, and instead of turning right, to go home, he turned left. It was as simple as that.

He walked.

He walked past the pub (a first), and on, out of the village. It just seemed like the thing to do. There was no reason. No plan. No destination. Just a packet of fags, and walking. The funny thing was that, once he had started, it made somehow made sense.

He continued walking, sleeping in hayricks, barns and people's houses, and after a week, he had arrived at the sea. He couldn't walk any further, but didn't want to turn round, so he got on a ship, signing on as a general hand on a merchant steamer, and off he sailed.

He had docked at several places, Famagusta, Aden, Calcutta, and each time, had got back on the ship, choosing to move on, until, one day, he arrived at Shanghai, and he got off.

"I sent you all a card from there, I remember."

He started walking again, and had got quite far into the Chinese countryside, when he was confronted by some local war lord-cum-bandit.

China had been under the control of war lords until nearly 1930, and they still held strong power and sway in some geographic areas. Their individual armies were gradually being integrated into the Kuomintang, which has the Chinese Nationalist Army, which was being mobilised to confront to invasion of Manchuria by Japan.

Into this situation, stepped Philip Holtom, a farm boy from Essex.

After a certain amount of discussion, Philip was presented to the local war lord, who was uncertain what to do with a wandering Englishman. He would quite happily kill him, but first he had to make sure that this Englishman wasn't important in some way, despite his appearance.

Having found someone that spoke (a minimal amount of) English and after a certain amount of debate, and tea being drunk, it was discussed that Philip could shoot. This was an extrapolation from his explaining that he was a farmer (they understood landowner), worked on the land and also shooting vermin and hunting for food (they translated warrior and soldier).

The war lord had no need for farmers, but he did need soldiers.

"Was it true that Philip was a soldier that could shoot?"

Philip, recognising a possible positive outcome from this tense discussion, admitted that, yes, he was in fact a soldier, who was quite famous in England.

"Good. Then you shall train my army how to use firearms," decided the war lord.

It seemed that the war lord had an army, and could muster thousands of men, if required, but they were peasants, armed with billhooks and scythes.

So Philip became a 'colonel' responsible for training a thousand Chinese peasants on how to shoot.

He had no actual basis or understanding of soldiering but he took his responsibility to heart and actually set up a military training regime, including marching, forming units, tactics, manoeuvring, and shooting. It turned out that this was something he was good at.

After all that walking, he finally seemed to have arrived.

The short story is that Philip commanded a company of men and led them against the Japanese as they tried to extend their presence from Manchuria into Eastern China. He excelled at his job and was rewarded handsomely, becoming the war lord's military advisor.

In the meantime, Chiang Kai-shek had gained control of all of the Chinese military, and the war lord (and Philip) were subsumed by the Kuomintang. In 1938, Philip became involved in the Sino-Japanese war

By the onset of WW2 (which was really a continuation of what he had been doing), Philip decided that his place would be by helping the British and he left and went to Malaya (the closest place with a British army).

When Japan had attacked and captured Singapore in 1942, he had found himself in Burma (now Myanmar). Half of Burma was pro-Japanese (or at least anti-British) and they formed a puppet government on the promise of independence after the war. Searching out the other half, that were pro-British, he set about creating a native resistance movement against the Japanese. It was just like being a war lord's military advisor again, but in the jungle.

The British, having lost their foothold in Malaya and Burma to the Japanese, tried to mount and create long range guerrilla wars against the Japanese, whilst they prepared for invasion. To do this, they dropped 'military advisors' (called Chindits) into the Jungle, with the objective of paying, and arming the local tribesmen.

On one such occasion, a British Chindit parachuted into a village, and told them that he could provide guns and ammunition.

"Oh, you need to go and see Mr Holtom. He's in the next village," he was told. And sure enough, he went over the hill and found Philip organising the locals to attack the invading Japanese.

"Yes, I would very much like some decent rifles, machine guns, claymores and ammunition," said Philip, and they provided them.

"And after the war, I was contacted by the Brits, and told to come down here, to Singapore, which is where you find me today," finished Philip.

"Bloody Hell," thought Giles. "A Holtom in the British Embassy. And, he's my uncle."

◆ ◆ ◆

As a post script to this meeting, we move forward to the mid 70's, when Philip Holtom and his Burmese wife, got off the plane at Heathrow, rang directory enquiries and was put through to Bill Holtom in Halstead.

"Hello. Is that Bill Holtom? The Bill Holtom who used to live in Gainsford End?"

"That's me," said Bill.

"This is your brother Phil. I'm at Liverpool street and will be there in 2 hours. Put the kettle on."

And so, after disappearing for 50 years, Phil had returned. He came for tea and stayed.

And so, Philip returned back to Essex, but it didn't last long. He only remained for about 6 months, then getting bored, Phil and his wife packed their bags one day and disappeared, never to be seen again.

I only heard about this after the fact, before I even had chance to actually meet him.

"You must be bored, after all of that fun in the Jungle, so I've decided that you are the man for a little job that's just come in," said Crisp wearing a smile that didn't reach his eyes.

"We want you to go to the White Pamirs," said the Captain. "It's just like your tours in Arabia, looking for anthrax and foot and mouth in the local animals, and a chance of good PR for the army."

"Oh, so long as the PR was good," thought Giles sarcastically. "Where the hell were the White Pamirs?"

The answer is Afghanistan – and West Pakistan (now Pakistan), and the USSR (now Tajikistan) and China. The Pamirs are a subrange of the Himalayan mountains and the meeting point for all of these countries.

"Oh, and you had better move fast. The valley is shut off by October, and you don't finish by then, you would be snowed in until the spring thaw."

It was July. Given that it might take anything up to a month to get there, this only left Giles about 6 weeks to do the job, or face staying until next March.

So, after nearly a month of travelling Giles arrived at Wakhan in the Pamir mountains, and this is where his "I was going to work on a yak" stories come from.

As I said, the Pamirs are at the juncture of 4 countries. This kind of thing is important for governments, but of very little interest to local herders, and absolutely no interest whatsoever to yaks, cows, sheep and goats, whose interest is that piece of grass, but not whether it is Afghani, Chinese or Pakistani grass.

This meant that Giles would be with tribesmen, crossing and re-crossing the borders, in search of flocks to test and check.

"The trick to riding a yak, is always pass on the inside," Giles was told. The reason is that yaks, when they come across one another, tend to be like bulls facing off, and they push the other yak out of the way. When the path is only 2 feet wide with a rock wall on one side and a sheer drop on the other, it is common for the 'outside' yak to be pushed over the edge. Just make sure that you're not sitting on it.

Strangely enough, given that he was in now freezing in the mountains, compared to roasting in the desert, the situations were remarkably similar.

The tribesmen welcomed Giles as an esteemed guest in just the same way as the Bedouins had. They slaughtered a lamb or goat to feast on and it was served on a mound of rice with flatbreads on a big brass plate. They called it ploff, and it is basically a dish of spiced mutton pieces chopped up into rice, and eaten with your hands. Ploff may be a bastardised form of what we now call pilaff.

An interesting part of his trip was when he met with Chinese and Russian border guards.

They were used to tribesmen walking past, herding a flock of goats, but it was certainly unusual to see a British soldier appear on a yak.

Initially it was a bit tense and strained, with rifles unslung from shoulders, and Giles' interpreter would then explain that he wasn't a one-man invasion, but a vet, come to check the animals.

Once introductions had been made, the soldiers would relax, and then sit down and offer some hospitality.

With the Chinese, this was tea, and with the Russians, this was, of course, vodka.

They each had a border post 'hut' with a brazier by the door to warm themselves by. They were so far from civilisation that they lived, ate and slept in their tiny hut. Giles got the impression that they were sent up here as a punishment, probably for a month at a time.

He imagined that in the winter the hut would be abandoned, after all, the passes were blocked with snow and nobody could get through anyway. Best leave it to the locals, eh.

Over the next few weeks, Giles would become a common visitor, as he crossed over the borders in search of herds to check. Once, they even set up an impromptu clinic for him to inspect the animals of some Chinese tribesmen from the next valley.

"Good PR for the army," thought Giles.

Giles had been invited down into the valley to meet and be a guest of a local Prince. He didn't know if this meant a Prince of the village, the valley, the region or of all Afghanistan, but a Prince nevertheless.

The Prince himself, spoke perfect English, and it turned out, had been educated at public school in Rugby.

"Do you like polo?" the Prince asked Giles. "We will show you proper polo - Buzkashi."

Buzkashi is basically like cage fighting, on horseback - with a goat.

From Giles' understanding, it consists of a group of men on horses. There are no teams and each man is for himself. The objective is to pick up the headless goat carcass and deliver it to a circle drawn on the ground at the other end of the field, all the while the other riders are beating, hitting and whipping you, trying to steal the carcass, so they can 'score' instead.

Giles was given a place of honour, sitting on the back of a flatbed truck with the Prince, watching the mayhem unfold.

The Prince provided Giles with a running commentary on the progress of the game.

"This is a jolly good rider," he would say. "From this village. Very strong. Oh. Pity. This is also a good rider."

All Giles could see was a moving melee of men's arms and horse's legs poking out of a thick cloud of dust.

"I suggest that discretion is the better part of valour," said the Prince, as the cloud thundered toward the flatbed. He and Giles hopped off behind the cab, as the leading horsemen jumped up, onto and over the truck, just where Giles had been sitting.

"Fine. Jolly fine," said the Prince.

Thank God, he was just about finished, and could go home, thought Giles.

On return to Singapore, Giles had another bout of malaria, probably brought on by the change in temperature (from 10C in Afghanistan to 40C in Singapore).

When he recovered from his delirium, he woke up to find a Captain Brown at the side of his bed. It was 100% humidity, so he didn't have a grey coat on. Nevertheless, he was definitely a Captain Brown.

"I understand you have been in and out of Russia and China," he said. "Perhaps you could answer a few questions about the state of the uniforms, morale, weapons," etc….

One day, we were all out shopping in Singapore, with my baby brother, Van, in his pram.

"I want to look at these chairs," said Liz, going into a shop. So Giles and I followed, leaving the pram outside.

"Guard," said Giles to Demon, who sat by the pram.

5 minutes later we came out to find Demon pinning some poor Malay down with her paws on his shoulders, and her jaws, poised, just above his face.

He was gibbering, as anyone would.

"Leave," Giles commanded (or maybe it was banana), and she moved back to her post by the pram.

Apparently, the man had looked in the pram, seen the cute baby and said, "what a cute little b…." and Demon had pinned him to the floor.

Luckily Giles had only said 'Guard'.

Demon was an excellent dog, and distinguished between Guard and Attack, whereas most dogs treated both as synonymous.

Now we come to the most important story in the book. Well, at least it is for me.

You see, this is the first memory I have in my life. My next is 2 years later and lasts 30 seconds, and I can only really remember my own life from about 6 years old – all apart from this incident, when I was not even three. But I can tell this story from the first person's viewpoint.

Giles came home one day and announced to me that "He had a big surprise for me."

He said surprise, but I heard present.

"Wow, my daddy has got me a present," I thought.

"It's at the base," he said, so we both got into his car.

It was a big American car, dark blue, with a huge bench seat in the front. I was so small, that I could only see the sky and the tops of palm trees through the windows, so I watched my daddy drive.

When they are very young, all children see their parents as gods. My daddy is the strongest. My mummy is the most beautiful. But at about 4 years old, we become develop the ability to be critical, and can see that Lucy's dad is more handsome, or Brian's mum is prettier.

I was not quite 3, and my daddy was handsome, with his tropical uniform (shorts), his peaked hat and his Ronald Coleman moustache – although to be fair, most men had Ronald Coleman moustaches at this time.

We arrived at the base, and I could see the gate guard salute my daddy (as he was so important), and I saw a red striped pole rise up, so we could drive in.

We got out of the car and walked to a building. It was a basha, which is like a monastery cloister, ie. 4 covered corridors around an open courtyard. We walked along one side and then around a corner, for me to see – a baby elephant.

"Wow," I thought, "My daddy has got me a baby elephant."

"Her name is Josephine. You can stroke her if you want," said Giles.

I walked up to her. She was lying on her tummy rather than standing, and so was almost exactly the same height as me. I stared at her, and she stared back through a big black eye. Her trunk came out to greet me, as I moved in to stroke her.

I ducked back to avoid this grey, dripping, snotty trunk. I hadn't moved fast enough and the trunk stroked me, leaving a snail's trail of mucus on my arm.

"Aaargh," I shrieked, and Giles laughed.

"She is a baby and won't hurt you. She just wants to sniff you and touch you – to be a friend. It's OK."

And so I stepped forward to be slobbered on and the trunk duly obliged.

Emboldened, I moved closer so that I could stroke her head, and discovered the most amazing thing. Elephant hair Is tougher, stronger and coarser than bristles on a bash broom.

It felt like stroking piano wires, and I expected them to 'plink' as my hand passed over them.

"What is that?" I asked.

"That's a belt to hoist her up, so she can stand without putting weight on her legs. Josephine has got polio, which is why we are looking after her."

We stayed for half an hour, with me allowed to feed her a little bit, and to sit and cuddle her, and talk to her, because she was 'poorly' and had 'poorlyo'.

"Time to go," announced my daddy, which is when it kicked off.

"Josephine is coming with us."

"I'm sorry. Josephine has to stay here."

I was adamant. My dad had promised me a present, and this was the best present ever, and she was going to come home with me.

Of course, it ended in tears, and I didn't get my elephant, but that's all I remember.

Apparently, when she was well, Josephine was bought by an American circus. If ever I go to an American circus, I bet she would remember me.

On return to base, Giles found Crisp gloating. "Sorry about your request for transfer. It has been denied," he said.

Giles had asked (several times) to be transferred to another unit, elsewhere. Ostensibly, to use his specific skills, but in reality, to get away from Crisp. This most recent one was to transfer to Hong Kong.

Each request had been denied, and Crisp made sure that Giles knew that it was him that had vetoed the move.

Captain Tom Derbyshire, RN, was a friend of Giles, they having been introduced by their respective wives.

Tom and his wife were saying their goodbyes as he was being posted to Hong Kong. And, sitting in Raffles, one evening, they discussed Giles predicament, and after a few Gins and tonic, and after a quick phone call with Captain (now Major) Spurry, who was in Hong Kong, a plan was hatched

Giles had guard duty. As a sergeant, he didn't actually have to guard anything. His job was to walk around the guard posts every 2 hours to check that the guard was still awake. Sleeping was a court martial offence. So was not checking on the guards, and on this particular evening, Giles didn't fulfil his duty, and didn't check the guard posts. He waited to be reported, so that Crisp would order a court martial, but nothing happened.

It seemed that the guards were covering for him. Which he didn't want to happen.

So, after waiting 2 days and hearing nothing, Giles mentioned that he hadn't done his guard inspection, in the hearing of a couple of Crisp's toadies.

Sure enough, within the hour, he was summoned to the office.

"Gross dereliction of duty. Asleep on guard, all in time of war (Ed: police action)," snarled Crisp, with barely hidden glee. "You are so fucked."

And so, Giles was court martialled and he was demoted back to the ranks.

He was also automatically transferred out of the unit. This is a standard regulation. The reason for this, is to prevent any demoted soldier, being in the same unit as before, where he might be subject to reprisals or bullying from men that he had previously commanded.

So Giles was transferred out to Hong Kong, and only 2 weeks later, he, Liz and his two kids, went aboard a ship bound for China.

On the dock, CSM Crisp, watched Giles leave. "I got you, you bastard," he mouthed, through the blast of the ship's horn, his face lit up with spiteful satisfaction.

Liz was furious. Court martialled and demoted. The shame of it, but Giles didn't seem to be taking it that badly.

The next day, Giles received a telex on board. Apparently, his new position in Hong Kong came with a promotion. He had embarked as a private, but would disembark in Hong Kong as a corporal. He was promoted back to sergeant within a year.

This is when he could tell Liz about the plan that Tom Derbyshire and John Spurry had put together. They knew that he would have to be transferred out (away from Crisp), and Spurry arranged that it would be back to him, in Hong Kong.

Meanwhile in the news:

Halstead Gazette
Local farm worker, Philip Holtom, found working in Singapore embassy.

14.   THE ROAD TO HONG KONG

Hong Kong was both the same as and completely different from Singapore.

Hong Kong, itself was not a major base, and there was no war or police action happening there. Instead, it was used as a hub from which Giles and his colleagues could be sent to different places to help out. So for him, it meant a lot of down time mixed with certain amount of travel.

For Liz, it was exactly the same social whirl as she had in Singapore, but perhaps even more extravagant and exclusive.

As before, they lived off base, in the New Territories in Kowloon. They had a nice top floor apartment overlooking Hong Kong below.

My brother tells me that on arrival in Hong Kong, Liz was pregnant, and in mid-1959, she gave birth to twins, a boy and a girl. Sadly, they lived less than 2 weeks. There is absolutely no record of this in either of Giles' or Liz's belongings. No photos, birth or death certificates. I don't remember this, but I was only 3½.

Liz decided that she wanted to do work of some kind, and got a part-time job as an English teacher. This filled her time, and it also gave her some money of her own, which she used to have some dresses made.

As in Singapore, hand made tailoring was cheap, so she could afford to design and create dresses that were wildly extravagant, and just for occasional use. She ended up with a set of Chinese silk dresses (called a Cheong Sam). These were the slim, figure-hugging dresses with the side slit up to the thigh or even higher.

Each one was designed using a different colour, so she had a collection of bright crimson, sky blue, emerald green and gold, available for any occasion. Each dress was covered in silk embroidery designs of dragons (red), swallows (gold), carp (green), and peacocks (blue).

I remember the blue dress. It had a single peacock with its head starting at the shoulder and then the body and tail feathers flowing around the dress to the floor. Each individual peacock feather was picked out with silver and gold thread with a single pearl sewn into the 'eye' of the feather.

This was the height of extravagance, but Liz could afford it, and it was expected of her as a member of the 'smart set'.

Whilst Liz was out teaching or socialising, Van and myself were looked after by an Amah. An Amah is a Chinese maid who cooks, cleans, irons and looks after the kids. Over the next 2 years, I learned to speak more Cantonese than English – although sadly, this has long gone.

The first trip Giles had was back to India, to go and supervise the purchase of mules for the army. He would check them over to see that they were good, usable animals, and then they would be shipped to either Egypt or Malaysia for use in the conflicts there.

The mules were in several different places, and so Giles had to travel through several cities (Delhi, Calcutta, Hyderabad) to see and check all of the animals.

In the end he had selected and authorised purchase for 500 mules, and was ready to get back to HK, when,..

This following story is a bit different. I only heard it once, when I was driving Giles back to Wales. It is incomplete as a whole story, just a fragment really, and came out as a non-sequitur and wasn't anchored to any other story or situation. Some parts don't make sense to me, but I never got the chance to clarify these with Giles.

I will tell it in the first person, just as Giles told me.

"I had to go to Nepal once."

"Really?" I asked. "I didn't know you had gone there. What was it like?"

"I had been in India buying mules for the army and was told to go to Nepal.

I went to the airport but they didn't have any flights. They only had 2 planes for that route, American DC10's from WW2, and one was damaged and the other was undergoing maintenance. I was told I would have to wait 10 days before the next flight.

I was sitting in the Nissen hut with the other passengers, there were about eight of us, and someone said, "I'm not waiting here for a week. Why don't we go there under our own steam?"

Nowadays you can take a car or bus, but in those days, to get to Nepal you walked or you flew, and so we all set off for Kathmandu on foot."

(Ed: as this is over 600 miles, I assume that they took other transport as well. My guess is a train to the nearest town and then perhaps by truck.)

"We hired some people to carry our luggage, and off we went. The road was a simple track, and easy to walk for the first part, and we all got along well.

I remember that most of the people were going to Nepal for some kind of business or other – for the army or British government, except a middle aged, English couple. The wife was the only woman in the group. They seemed to be doing it for some kind of holiday, which was very rare in those days.

Holidays were Scarborough and Bridlington, not Kathmandu, and certainly not on foot.

Anyway, all the walking was not that bad, as the first part was quite flat, and we had people carrying our stuff. There were villages with restaurants and rooms to stay in.

The last 50 miles was uphill, and things got much harder. Now the route, was just a track, and nothing more. In those days, there weren't many (if any) roads usable by cars and lorries. Great for donkeys. The villages were further apart and more and more rural.

There was no chance of getting a hotel room, as there were no hotels. We simply stayed in barns, and sometimes, in people's houses.

And then the villages and houses ran out.

This was the part of the trip that looked just like the assault on Everest, that had happened just a few years before. The track went through passes, over mountain ridges and across the raging torrents flowing along the valley floors.

To me, it was just like my time in the Pamirs, with rocky paths, only a couple of feet wide, with dizzying drops on one side.

Sometimes the bottom of the valley we were crossing was quite wide and flat, and here, the river was usually fordable on foot. And you would pick your way, from rock to rock, through freezing meltwater that was anywhere from your below your knees to above your waist. You often had a rope to hang on to, to stop you being washed away.

But the thing I remember most was the bridges. They had bridges when the river was too deep to ford and the valley floor was narrow, more like a cleft in the mountain, with water rushing by below.

There were two types of bridges; those that seemed to go from one peak to another, swaying across a dizzying, booming gorge, far below, and those that were low and only about 10-20 feet above the water.

The high bridges were simple rope affairs, and looked identical to those in Indiana Jones. Sometimes, they were basically three ropes, forming a 'V', the bottom, thick bundle of ropes on which you stepped, and one either side, used as handrails. The better ones had actual wooden slats for your feet. The scary part was the height above the gorge (DON'T LOOK DOWN!), as the wind would push at you and cause the whole bridge to sway, and it was easy to get dizzy.

The lower bridges were the same as the higher ones, except that the sound was horrendous, and you couldn't hear what the next person was shouting when he was only 2 yards away from you, and often you couldn't see very well because the boiling water below sent up a spray that formed a wall of mist, that gave you the most amazing rainbows all around you, but you couldn't see the other side. The hand rails and wooden slats were all slick with spray.

It was on one such bridge that we lost the wife. She just slipped and fell in.

Everybody got to the other side, and the porters immediately scrambled over the rocks on both sides of the river, searching for over a mile downstream. They never found the body.

We were all a bit numb with shock. The person who seemed the least affected was the husband. He didn't seem to be too concerned by his wife's loss, and said, "There's nothing we can do here. Let's carry on.", and so we did, and 2 days later, we walked into Kathmandu."

◆ ◆ ◆

Whilst Giles was away in India and Kathmandu, Liz was still out enjoying her social life.

During the day, she would meet up with the wives and play mahjongg or canasta. Sometimes it was, out with the kids to picnic at Lion rock, or a day spent swimming at Silver strand beach.

And in the evening, as she didn't drive, one of the men would pick her up and escort her to the cocktail parties, downtown or over on the peak.

Sometimes they would all go to Happy Valley races, and the host (usually Chinese) would hand out little packs of tokens to the women, so they could bet on the races.

Liz was in her element, as she might arrive on the arm of John Spurry or Tom Derbyshire, or sometimes both (a Major and a Captain!).

She would drink Daiquiris, Mai Tais and smoke Sobranie cocktail cigarettes, using a holder. She was in social heaven.

It could never be better than this.

There was only one bad situation to mar this idyll, and it happened like this.

Liz was at a party in someone's house, when she stepped into the bedroom to repair her make up. In the room was a visiting

American Captain, who was sitting on the bed having a quiet drink, when he spun round to see Liz applying lipstick.

He got, fresh, as the Americans say, and made a move on Liz.

"C'mon Honey. Let's see a little of that special relationship," he urged, as he grabbed Liz and tried to force his hand up her skirt. She slapped him as hard as she could and left the room.

Nothing more was said, and the Captain was still invited to parties for the next couple of months of his stay in HK.

You see in those days, if she complained, the men would sympathise, but dismiss it thinking, "Nothing really happened,", "It was only a bit of fun,", "Hell, he was probably a bit drunk.", "Giles was away and she was probably asking for it."

The women on the other hand would ostracise her on the spot, "What was she doing, being with him in the bedroom anyway?", "She brought it on herself,", "I always thought she was a bit flighty.".

No matter what she did, he would probably get off Scot free, and she would be branded as the women who 'asked for it'.

Liz hated Americans from this day onward.

Back in Hong Kong, Giles slipped into this social whirl, alongside Liz, unaware of the situation with the American. She didn't tell him until they had left Hong Kong.

Without the travel, Giles had to report for duty each day, but this often meant nothing more than just sitting in the office or a guard house for 8 hours.

He, and a friend Steve Benbow, decided to learn the guitar. They would split the price of guitar lessons between them, to make it cheaper.

Giles knew more about Guitars than Steve, as he knew they had 6 strings. Steve thought they had 5. They went into town and each bought a second-hand guitar for a few dollars and started their lessons.

Learning Guitar is an excellent hobby, especially when you have 8 hours to kill, sitting in a guard house, 3 days a week.

Pretty soon, both got quite good, and would play at parties together. They even went down to a booth where you could play your own songs, and make a record. Somewhere in the pile of junk that used to be Giles' belongings, there is a copper and wax disk of "Hernando's Hideaway".

Later in life, Steve continued with his guitar playing, and he became quite famous on the folk circuit, even having a hit single in the charts and played on Top of the Pops.

One day, Giles was asked to do an interview for Hong Kong Radio, explaining for their listeners, what the veterinary corps did.

He had taken me along, and during his interview, the technicians had left the studio, to go and play football with me, outside in the courtyard.

When the interview was finished, the DJ asked Giles if he could 'hold the fort' whilst he joined his pals for a kick about.

He was instructed, "Press this button to hear the disk on the left, and this button to hear the one on the right. Use this slider to transmit and mute your voice. Easy. There are some records lined up over there. Choose what you want to play."

And so for half an hour Giles talked and played some records. It was easy and fun to do.

Interestingly, the station received several calls, saying that they like the new DJ, and so he was asked to come back and DJ Giles was born. He got paid $30 a show, which was quite a lot of money in those days.

Giles did have to do a little veterinary work. Local (Brits) would bring their pets in to be checked/fixed. For example, one day he was faced with a distraught lady and her pet budgie.

"I think it has a broken wing."

"How did that happen?" asked Giles.

"He fell out of the window."

"But surely he can fly?"

"Yes, but he was in his cage at the time."

Giles bit his bottom lip to prevent himself from laughing, whilst in his head, he had a vision of that new Tweety bird cartoon with the bird flapping desperately, trying to keep its cage aloft as it plunged to the ground.

"I'll see what we can do," he said.

Giles and Liz received an invitation to the wedding of the season.

One of the Chinese couples that they would meet at parties were getting married, and it turned out that daddy was a millionaire (when a million was a lot of money).

The wedding was designed to be ostentatious and to show off the wealth of the couple's families.

After the ceremony, they all sat down to a 14-course wedding lunch of exquisite and exotic Chinese food.

Giles was sat between two Chinese matrons, who generally ignored him and conversed with the people on either side of them. He concentrated on eating and enjoying the food.

One course was a single, large prawn with some sauce and a green 'thing'. He didn't want to be seen as uncouth or impolite, and so after eating the prawn, set about tackling the green thing. It resisted his knife, so in the end, he had to pop it, whole, into his mouth.

It was like eating a bath plug.

The problem was, that the thing wouldn't go away. He chewed and chewed, to no avail, and finally, after taking a swig of wine, he gulped and swallowed it, whole.

"What was that we just had?" he enquired of the lady to his right.

"Prawn," she replied.

"No. I meant the green thing."

"Oh. That was garnish. Just to make the plate look nice. It was a raw duck's foot. You didn't eat it did you?"

"No. No. I just wondered what it was," said Giles as he dropped his napkin over the plate to hide the fact that it had gone.

After each alternate course, the bride, would get up, and go and change. Appearing after 5 minutes in another dress, of a different colour.

She wore 7 different dresses throughout the wedding lunch, before they left to change and prepare for the evening's party and festivities.

The family wanted to show that they were rich, and they had succeeded.

"That was amazing," said Liz.

"Do you remember the prawn dish with the green thing?" asked Giles.

"The duck's foot? Yes. Why? You didn't eat it did you?"

"Me? Of course not. I'm not a fool."

Drunk driving was quite common in those days. People accepted it as a norm in the same way as casual sexism and racism was. In any case, the police always let you off. Especially in Hong Kong, where 90% of the HK Force, were ex-metropolitan police.

And so, Major Spurry meandered his way over to his car, after a night of cocktails at a house on the peak.

The Peak, as the name infers, is a high mountain in the centre of Hong Kong Island. It was mostly wooded, with a very few, rich residences situated off to the side of the windy, mountain road.

"I'll drive, lieutenant," he announced, and the lieutenant, knowing what was good for him, sat in the passenger seat.

"See you at the bottom," he said, as the car lurched out of the driveway.

Giles and Liz hopped into their own car and gave chase, following the tail lights as they rolled off down the hill.

On each hairpin bend, the lights would disappear out of sight for a second, and then come back into view as Giles also made it round the corner. And then all of a sudden, they weren't.

"Christ. He's gone off the side." And sure enough he had.

There were precious few barriers, and just the occasional post to mark the edge of the road. Nine out of ten times, the crash would have been fatal, with the car plunging a 100 feet down a cliff face. But in this case, Giles stopped the car, looked over the edge, to find the car wedged on its side in a tree.

The window wound down and John Spurry emerged, standing up to his waist, through the opening.

"Are you OK?"

"Perfectly fine. Not a scratch."

"I'll get help to pull you out," said Giles, as a couple of cars full of the other party guests arrived onto the scene.

Liz noticed that the whole of Spurry's body, from the waist up, was sticking out of the car.

"What are you standing on?"

"Nothing."

The nothing turned out to be the lieutenant, and John Spurry was standing on his head, but he was a lieutenant and knew better than to say anything.

Both were fished out and put in the back of a partygoer's car. The drunk Major and the lieutenant with the boot print on his cheek.

"I'll get someone to come and pick up the car tomorrow," said Spurry, giggling, as he waved and was driven off.

We had spent the afternoon at Silver strand beach, and I had got badly burnt. I have very fair skin and had gone out without a T shirt to cover me.

In the end, they had to take me to the hospital, where it was found that I had 3rd degree burns. Basically, it was similar to pouring petrol over myself and setting light to it.

It was around this time, that Giles asked Liz what she thought about the future. He had less than a year to go in his original 13-

year contract with the army, and a decision to re-enlist or not was coming up soon.

For Giles, it was an easy decision. He loved his work. He found it easy and interesting, and he couldn't think of any other job that would give him opportunities like this. He would sign on for another 13 years, taking him up to the maximum, and giving him an excellent pension, whilst still being in his forties.

For some reason, maybe it was the American, who knows? But Liz said that she wanted to go home, and so, in deference to her wishes, Giles submitted that he wouldn't be re-enlisting.

Oh, well, thought the army. If you don't want to stay, then you should come back to the UK, to serve out your last year, and so, Giles and Liz left Hong Kong, and returned to the UK.

Liz to Yorkshire, to find a house, and Giles back to Melton Mowbray, before he too, moved up to Dewsbury, and the new house in Healds Road that Liz had found.

All of the other experienced vets were abroad, in Malaya, Egypt, Aden, etc., so the army gave him one last job to do. They wanted him to ride in the Horse of the Year show at Olympia, representing the British Army.

He was going to be on telly.

In 1961, the Horse of the Year show was big television. It was a big event, attracting riders from all over the world, rivalling Saturday Night at the Palladium for popularity.

The format would be to show jump a round, and then for the top 12 riders to jump another new layout. This time against the clock, to determine the winner.

The initial round was difficult, as they wanted only the best and most accomplished riders to have clear rounds. It consisted of sets of jumps, some singles, some in pairs and one set of three jumps, one after another (a treble), giving the horse and rider only a single step between landing and jumping the next fence.

Olympia was a large convention space, used for car shows, boat shows, and the modern homes exhibition. When set up for HoYS, the ring itself was only about 60 yards long by twenty wide, so it was very compressed compared to outside venues.

Backstage there was a practise area with a couple of jumps, where a horse and rider could warm up before they went into the ring.

Giles didn't like his horse, Goldie, much. The veterinary corps had many horses, but none that were international show jumping standard and it had been provided by some other regiment. It was a headstrong stallion that he had not ridden before.

In the warm up ring it had jumped big, which means that it cleared the fences with lots to spare, but it also meant that it needed to be reined in, was too eager, and didn't listen well to his inputs.

He thought that it probably wouldn't react well to the noise and glare in the ring, but it is a poor workman who blames his tools, and this was the horse the army had given him.

"Representing the British Army, Sergeant Giles Holtom of the Royal Army Veterinary Corps," boomed the tannoy, and off he went.

In Yorkshire, Liz and her family were avidly watching this on their TV in the front room.

"Mum, come quick. He's on."

The objective of the first round was to get through without knocking over any fences. He had no time constraints, so the strategy would be to take each jump carefully and in a controlled manner, and all went according to plan, with Goldie responding well to Giles' control over the singles and doubles. With just the treble left, he only had 4 faults. All that was left was the three fences and the few steps to the finish.

He knew it had gone wrong by the second fence, as the horse leapt so big that he didn't have the proper space for the step before the third fence. Nevertheless the horse made it, and even cleared it well, but there was no stopping the bloody horse now and it charged along the side of the arena, past the turn for the finish, and straight on toward the barriers at the end, which it also cleared, landing in the orchestra pit.

"Sergeant Holtom disqualified," said the announcer, in his plummy voice.

So it was definitely time to leave the army, thought Giles. Maybe he could get to Yorkshire before any of his mates would hear about this.

Meanwhile in the news:

Halstead Gazette
Local boy, Giles Holtom, on TV tonight, riding in Horse of the Year Show.

15.   AND SO, IN CONCLUSION

W hen I started to write this, the intention was simply to make sure that the stories Giles had told me and my brothers were not lost.

In writing them, I had to do a certain amount of research, which put some flesh and background to the stories, so now in some cases, they were not just silly little anecdotes, but full-fledged adventures.

The second part of this effort came when I sat down with Giles a few years before he died. At this time, he finally told me some of the background to his stories, and answered questions, that had never occurred to me as a small boy.

My first question was, "how on earth was it possible for a single, British Soldier to wander through all of these countries, armed with a revolver and his kit bag, and not get into trouble? Surely you would have been kidnapped or shot at?"

"This was not long after the war," said Giles, "and Britain was generally viewed positively. So I was usually safe."

"On the other hand, if some local hotheads decided to try and kidnap me, a wiser person would point out that the British army would send a regiment to get me back, and they didn't want that kind of trouble. Best lend me a donkey and let me go on."

"Finally, I was often a guest and under the protection of a local chief, lord, or Prince, and that also guaranteed my safety. So, I managed to wander through situations without any real trouble. Of course, it would be different nowadays."

Two main things came out of our discussions; CSM Crisp and the Men in Grey Coats. I had never really heard about either before.

There are questions that come out of these revelations. Specifically, how much influence did Crisp and/or the men in grey coats have on Giles' career.

Did CSM Crisp really try to send Giles to places so he might be in harm's way and get killed?

Well, I can say with certainty that Crisp was known to several people in the corps as a paedophile, but Giles' army colleagues, that I have spoken to, all said that he had a special dislike for Giles.

It is also fairly certain that an CSM has a lot of influence and power over which soldier gets what duties, even if directed by a senior officer. Examples might include;

"Holtom has applied for this transfer and I think that's a good idea. Don't you agree Sergeant?"

"I don't think he's ready yet sir."

Or perhaps, "Who can we put forward for this job in Addis Ababa?"

"I know just the man sir."

Giles did tell me three things about Crisp; that he had discovered his secret and had thus made an enemy of him, that Crisp delighted in sending him on dangerous or uncomfortable missions, and was equally frustrated when Giles came back alive, and sometimes commended, and finally, he told me the story behind his court martial to get out from under Crisp's influence.

The remainder of CSM Crisp that you see in this book are my own extrapolations from these pieces of information.

◆ ◆ ◆

The other part that is interesting, to me, is the involvement of the "Men in Grey Coats".

Giles only ever mentioned them a couple of times, once after Austria and once after his detour in Yugoslavia, and even then he only said the bare minimum about them. Ostensibly naming them, "Men in Grey Coats" or people that we don't talk about. After all, he was in the army, and he had signed the official secrets act.

This bare minimum leaves large areas to be filled, and it is my opinion that the men in grey coats had quite an influence upon Giles' career. Probably as much as Crisp ever did.

Why do I say this?

Well, they certainly got Giles out of a couple of courts martial (or at least severe reprimands).

It is inconceivable that a soldier can go AWOL in Vienna for 6 months and not receive any disciplinary action. The same must be said for Giles wandering into Yugoslavia and missing his posting to Korea. In each case Crisp was dancing with fury as Giles was let off, and even thanked for his actions.

By the same token, if the men in grey coats wanted something, then it is highly likely that the normal army would comply. For example;

"We think it would be good if Sergeant Holtom went on the language training course," or, "We require you to send Sergeant

Holtom to East Berlin."

Which meant they could have theoretically had as much effect as Crisp upon the direction and outcomes of Giles' career.

For my own part, I believe that Army Intelligence used Giles as an unwitting dupe. He wasn't a spy. Spies are people that can, as part of their profession, dissimulate. As the saying goes, to obtain trust, you need to be sincere, and once you can fake that, you've got it made.

Giles certainly wasn't good spy material. He was too open and innocent. People naturally liked and trusted him, which was certainly to his advantage, but if he had been asked to play a part, and dupe someone or fake sincerity, he would have certainly have failed. It wasn't in his nature. So the MIGC had to rely upon Giles not knowing something, rather than knowing and being able to hide it.

He was always open and genuine, sometimes even stupid and agricultural rather than refined and clever and people felt that. But this very innocence and openness worked in his favour.

The Russians certainly though he was a spy. But on meeting him, they rapidly came to the conclusion that he was actually a vet, who had come to help fix their rabies problem.

That being said, Giles was very intelligent and observant and the MIGC relied on this. He could provide them with lots of information without having to be officially part of the team.

So, who was it that directed Giles' career, Crisp or the MIGC?

Personally, I like to think that it was probably a bit of both. I can see CSM Crisp sending Giles to Korea (war), Crete (rabies), the desert (maximum discomfort and danger), and the Malayan jungles (malaria).

I can also see the MIGC sending Giles to East Berlin, Addis Ababa, the desert (2nd tour), Afghanistan and language school.

But, knowing Giles, it may just have been chance and serendipity. Who knows?

"Hmmm. It is a hard decision on who to send to the Korean conflict. I can't decide. They are all some mother's son," said Lieutenant Spurry. "I know. We will choose the next person to come through that door."

Knock, knock.

"Ah, Holtom. Come in. I have an assignment for you."

PART II: DECLINE, FALL AND RISE.

Of course Giles' life didn't stop there in 1961. He went on to live until his eighties, but his life was never to the same level or as concentrated as with his life in the Army. Not only that, the protagonists are different and there are no baddies driving the narrative, other than Giles and Liz themselves.

This doesn't mean that and it was not filled with achievements and controversies. It is just that there are no yaks or lions involved.

It does however, involve Giles going to prison, coming 3rd in a world championship, obtaining a Doctorate and turning down a Professorship, Princess Anne telling dirty jokes, two divorces and celebrating 30 years happily not married.

16.   WHAT HAPPENED NEXT?

Dewsbury was a mill town. It had collieries nearby, but the town sat astride the river Calder and was filled with cloth mills.

The local stone was a honey limestone, but every single building was black. Dyed with the smoke and soot from mines, mills, factories and coal fires. It was a black, grimy town.

In 1961 the mills were still working. They took water out of the river Calder, passed it through the mill, to clean, dye, and rinse the cloth, and then put the dirty, dyed, sudsy water back into the river. Sometimes the froth could be 6 feet deep, and gusts of wind would blow clumps of thick, sticky suds off the river to fly over the roofs of the surrounding houses and into the playgrounds of the local schools.

It was common for clothing, left outside on the line to dry, to come in dirtier than when it went out.

Liz had done well, and chosen a quite posh house in a nice part of town, on top of a hill out of the centre. It was a large, 4 bed, Victorian mansion with an open park space in front and backing onto the playing fields of the girl's high school.

In 1962, when Giles arrived from Melton, he was given a job by Liz's father, Rex, working as a man from the Pru.

The 'Man from the Pru' was an institution that was respected and trusted implicitly, in most cases, more than a bank. In fact many people had policies with the Pru (Prudential Insurance) and no bank account.

In those days, many people, especially from poorer families paid for insurances (life, funeral, car) on a weekly or monthly basis, and the man from the Pru would come around each week, with his satchel and collect the premiums from the house wives.

For some, unknown, reason, Giles just couldn't be bothered. He needed a job, and this was an easy one, that paid well, but he couldn't motivate himself.

For the last 13 years, the army had told him when to shit, shower and shave. They ordered and controlled his life. He wanted for nothing. They provided food, housing, work, entertainment, in fact everything, and now when Giles had to do this on his own and under his own steam, he couldn't. He would have to learn how to function in normal society (rather than in the military).

He was lethargic, would get up late, and miss appointments and meetings. After a few months he was sacked, to the embarrassment of Rex and Liz.

For her part, I believe Liz was also depressed. She had come from exotic Hong Kong, with maids, cocktails and handmade dresses to a grimy and dour Yorkshire.

The problem was that, even though it was her home town, she didn't know anyone, and had no friends. In contrast to Germany, Singapore and Hong Kong, where there were army wives, who gathered around you, forming an instant support group and society, in Yorkshire, there was no-one apart from her parents. She had no friends. She hadn't seen them for 13 years and they were all married, with kids, and had moved on. She was in no club or group with common interests. People played whist not canasta and they drank black beer shandy, not Mai Tais.

The only option for her was the old Ebenezer Baptist church socials, which offered fish paste sandwiches and cups of tea. A far cry from martinis and canapés at Raffles.

I don't have a great memory of this time, regarding Giles and Liz, as I was just 6, and these things happened around me but were never discussed.

In 1964, after just over a year, we moved from the Victorian mansion in Dewsbury to a smaller 3 bedroomed new house in Huddersfield. It was a step down, but Van and I, as kids, didn't really feel it as much as Giles and Liz.

At this point, I believe Giles had bought a newsagent's shop in Ravensthorpe. He was his own master, and so didn't have to comply with rules and meetings set by a boss, but he was still subject to commitments – to open the shop at 6am, prepare the newspapers for delivery, then serve in the shop, until he closed, late in the evening.

The work was mind numbingly dull, and he hated the job. He wouldn't be able to stick this for long, and yet he did, day in day out, 12-14 hours a day, 6 days a week.

During this time, how I don't know, Giles became interested in Gliding, and we spent many weekends at Halifax Gliding club. For Van and I this meant exploring and roaming across hillsides with kids from the other members.

Giles became hooked on Gliding, and studied everything he could about the sport. He even qualified for his Bronze C, which is the third highest Gliding certification you can get (ultimately obtaining his Silver C, which is the highest qualification possible in the UK).

For her part, Liz liked it less, but in the end she enjoyed it, as it gave her access to a new group of women friends – the Glider pilot's wives, and so, the day trips to go flying lasted longer, as Giles and Liz stayed on after, in the flying club, drinking and socialising.

In 1965, after just another year, we moved again, from Huddersfield back to Dewsbury. This time we moved into a 2 up, 2 down, end-terrace, factory house in Saville Town, which was just by the mills.

The was another step down, to the bottom rung of the ladder, and even Van and I noticed the difference, but it didn't affect us much, as we easily made friends and were immediately happy.

Giles sold the newspaper shop in Ravensthorpe and started a new shop in Dewsbury, to repair sewing machines. He called it 'Vanmar', which I disliked, because he had put Van's name before mine. It should have been 'Marvan'.

This didn't last long as a venture. It seemed that women no longer made their own clothes. Bespoke tailors and dressmakers were going out of business. There had been a revolution in the clothing industry and off the rack clothes were filling all of the shops. It seems that selling and repairing sewing machines was similar to fixing buggy whips, in the age when people were buying cars not horse buggies..

It should be noted that from about 1960 to 1965, the British government had advertised abroad, in the commonwealth, for workers to come and work in the UK, to help with our economic recovery and growth.

In Dewsbury, we had mills and they required workers, and a great many of the jobs had been taken by Pakistanis. They had grouped together, taking over certain areas of the town, which became Pakistani suburbs, and where we lived in Saville town was directly neighbouring one such area.

I was unaware of any problem with this. We even had Pakistani kids in our school – albeit only a couple at that time. But this is the first time I noticed that Liz was strongly racist.

As a child I found it hard to understand.

We had lived out whole lives up to that point in foreign countries, with Germans, Malays, and Chinese, and Liz had never had a problem, but here, back at home, she hated them, especially 'Pakkis'.

It seemed that Liz's racism was directly linked to the colour of a person's skin. Chinese were OK, Malays, not so much, Pakistanis and Indians were 'dirty' and Negroes (even though we had never met any) were beyond consideration.

It was something that we argued about, throughout her life. As she got older, she would bite her tongue, but not saying anything didn't mean that she had changed her opinion, just that she kept it to herself.

As I grew older, the tension between Giles and Liz became more apparent, even to a child. Liz would complain about Giles throwing our money around on Gliding, when we couldn't make ends meet. At the same time, she was still trying to maintain the image of a certain level of social standing which we simply didn't have. For her, this was made worse by living next door to 'bloody immigrants'.

The only light in this dark situation was provided by the occasional visits from old army colleagues. (Uncle) Ted Simmons came up from his home in Somerset and would stay for a weekend. We would go out for a Chinese meal.

For us, it was a nostalgic reminder of a previous life, but for 99% of the population, it was the latest craze, and Chinese restaurants were springing up in every town in the country.

Tom Derbyshire had also left the Navy and moved back to Yorkshire, just the other side of Dewsbury, so he was another old pal that we often went over to see (but never invited to where we lived).

In four years, we had moved three times, starting at the top and ending at the bottom of the housing ladder. This drop in status was desperately hard for Liz to come to terms with.

In her bedroom, she still had a hand carved chest, lined with camphor wood, to protect her hand-embroidered, silk cocktail dresses. The zenith of her life had passed and she would never wear them again.

Liz and Giles' relationship soured. Their life had got much worse since he had the Army. We were poor, and neither parent had a job. So they did what many people did with broken relationships, they tried for another baby. Yes, that will sort out the problems. Maybe we will finally get that girl we wanted.

And on January 1st 1966, my brother Julian was born in Dewsbury General Hospital.

Maybe this was a sign. Things would get better now, wouldn't they?

I woke up one day, a few months later, to find that Giles had gone. I was 10. Van was 7 and Julian was 6 months old.

I won't say much about this period, because these stories are about Giles' life, and he wasn't there.

It was a time of massive recriminations, with Liz repeatedly stating that "Everything is your father's fault," and "He is a bastard who has just run off and left us." This was echoed by Liz's mother Edith.

Nobody told Van or me anything, other than "Your father has run away and left you alone."

We didn't know why he had left, where he had gone, if he would come back or when.

And so, we found ourselves living on social security. I was soon to realise the massive stigma attached to this.

The social security system had been around for a while, but it wasn't the safety net it later became. To be on the 'social' you had to be absolutely destitute, and the government, the media and all of your friends treated you as though they were doing you a big favour by allowing you to receive it.

In the 60's, society was changing rapidly, most particularly in terms of women's equality and position in society. For, although it had a long way to go before it reached today's situation, it was nevertheless a major social upheaval.

1. Women had the pill, and could control their own reproductive system. This meant many women could have sex, without the fear of getting pregnant, whereas previously they would have fallen pregnant and then have to marry the father. One mistake could see you committed to a relationship for life. Now it wasn't so.

2. Women were increasingly a factor in the workplace. They had worked during the war, but had been pushed back

into the kitchen by the returning soldiers, and society hoped that it could return to the social situation of the 30's, where men worked and were the bread winners and women cooked their meals and looked after the children. Instead, women were increasingly competing for men's jobs and working alongside them.

3. Divorces were starting to happen. Divorce had always been possible, but in reality, it was unheard of. The divorce rate of the 50's was negligible, and the 60's was the turning point when this started to happen. Today (in 2020), over 50% of marriages end in divorce, whereas then, it was more like 5%.

All of these circumstances came together to create change and form new situations in society. Single mothers had all of a sudden, become a phenomenon. One that nice society didn't like.

It didn't like this at all.

The Daily Mail repeatedly ran stories of single mothers 'sponging' off society, who didn't work and were given luxury homes by the council. They received so much money that they didn't have to actually work, and all of this was being paid for by OUR taxes!

Single mothers, with children, on benefits was the new point of scorn and revulsion, and until the Daily Mail moved on to the 'war on drugs' then 'Immigrants' and more recently 'Refugees', Liz, Van and I were one case in point.

I was only 10. I didn't work. I wasn't married and so, if I think about it, my life was not massively affected, except for two things; the social security services and my Grandma.

To claim social security you had to prove need, and the government was very suspicious. They believed that every applicant was lying in order to obtain benefits under false pretences.

So Liz had to prove that Giles had run away. Which is hard, as it was trying to prove a negative.

She was subject to frequent visits by inspectors, who came around unannounced, hoping to find Giles hiding behind the settee. Once they were satisfied that Giles had actually skipped off, then they switched to checking to see if Liz had a boyfriend who 'stayed over', and could therefore be considered a partner, again relieving Liz of the need for claiming benefits.

On a couple of occasions, my dad's friend, Ted Simmons, had visited, to make sure we were OK. Liz had to ask him to move his car during the evening, as social security inspectors would come past, note the car outside the house, and put a penny on the rear wheel. They would come past in the morning to see if the penny was still there, proving that the car had not moved overnight.

At the same time, the social security had also decided that I would be a good source of information.

I would be called out of class by the headmaster, Mr Howells.

He started off by sympathising, "You are the man of the household now. You have to be brave."

Then he would ask me "When did you last see your father?"

Yes. Just like the painting, and with the same objective and implication.

On the one hand I had Liz telling me not to say anything and on the other the headmaster questioning me on visitors to the house. I found this very terrifying and stressful.

"What if I said something wrong? Would mum go to jail and Van, Julian and I would be alone?"

The other thing that happened in school was Free Dinners. Children of parents that were poor did not have to pay 5 shillings (25p) a week for school dinners.

Each Monday. During registration, the teacher would call out each person's name and they would troop up to the front to hand over the dinner money.

Each week, the teacher would call out my name, pause for a second, and loudly state, "Oh. Yes, Free Dinners," thus (re)stating to the whole world that my family couldn't afford the 5 shillings to pay for the dinners.

Grandma Edith was an uncompromising lady. She had lived through 2 world wars, rationing, poverty and hard work. She wasn't a bad person, but she was a product of her generation and upbringing. She was thoroughly traditional and unforgivingly conservative in her outlook.

On the one hand, her Christian views forced her to help Liz, but this didn't stop her voicing her opinions and views, repeatedly, loudly and often. Her charity was a kind of blackmail. To receive it you had to run the gauntlet of her disapproval.

Liz said that we needed new shoes and she had no money, so Edie said she would buy them. But not before she had said, "I'm only buying these because your good for nothing father has run away and left you, leaving me and your Granddad to take care of you. You should be grateful to us for what you get."

She had to pick the shoes, so that we didn't waste the money. I wanted a snazzy pair that I had seen on TV. She bought us both pairs of brown plastic sandals. The plastic was so hard it left welts and blisters where the sandal rubbed on your feet – but the soles were good for 20,000 miles of walking.

We had a rented TV, but the shop repossessed it for non-payment. Now, to watch TV, we would have to go to Grandma's, and she would not allow us to watch programmes that we wanted, like the Monkees. Instead, we were forced to watch Songs of Praise with Thora bloody Hird.

Despite the regular third degree from Mr Howell, the stigma of poverty and free dinners and the repeated sermonising of my Grandma, life wasn't really that hard, and I survived it with no more than the usual mental scars.

I passed my 11+ and became a Grammar school boy.

It was in the spring of 1968, that Liz told me that Dad had been found. I was sworn to secrecy, and told not to tell anyone, including Van.

Apparently, Uncle Ted (Simmons) had heard about Giles from a mutual friend and tracked him down to Lasham, a gliding club near Basingstoke. He was living as a gliding bum, which I imagine is like a surf bum but without the waves.

Ted had negotiated some reconciliation between Giles and Liz, and one day, a few weeks later, I woke up and Giles was home.

All I knew was what I had been told, repeatedly over the last 2 years; he was a lazy, untrustworthy, feckless, useless man, who had run away rather than face his responsibilities, and look after his wife and children.

I didn't know what to say, and so nothing was said. It was never discussed. I never knew why he had gone, where he had been, what he had done.

I was 12 years old, and thankfully, I was no longer the man of the household.

Liz and Giles had got back together, but life hadn't really changed. We were still as poor as ever. So they did what many people did when trying to repair broken relationships, they decided on a new start. Somewhere else, away from those local busybodies, and sermonising family.

Liz was applying for several jobs as a nurse. She hadn't worked for over 15 years, but had managed to get her license status renewed, and started looking. She would scan the nursing times each month, applying for jobs all over the UK. Part of the attraction was that it would take them away from Dewsbury, which they believed was the source of their problems.

Later that year, Liz was accepted for a job as a district nurse in Eastbourne. It was a new start, and it came with a council house.

So, we moved to Eastbourne.

17. BESIDE THE SEASIDE, BESIDE THE SEA (A NEW LIFE)

Eastbourne is a town in Sussex on the south coast of England.

It was a pale sibling of Brighton, just down the road, which had received Royal patronage in the 18th century. Brighton was 'little London' whereas, by contrast, Eastbourne was God's waiting room. British people retired there in their scores, and it had the second largest population of old age pensioners in Britain, losing the title to Bexhill, just down the coast.

Old people came to Eastbourne to die, and then forgot why they came there.

Despite all of this, compared to Dewsbury, it was a great place for our family. We had a nice, three bed council house in a decent area, and both Van and I had friends and went to good schools.

Giles took a job as a lorry driver, working for a company called Hall & Co. Mostly he was delivering gravel and shingle for use in building. Not a very taxing job, but it brought in money and he was happy.

Liz had become a local district nurse. This is a nurse that visits patients in their own home instead of at a surgery or in hospital.

In order to do her rounds, as she didn't know how to drive a car, the council provided her with a Raleigh Wisp moped with the outlandish top speed of about 22mph.

A large part of her work was administering insulin to elderly diabetics or looking after pensioners that had had hip replacement surgery, which was being pioneered in a local hospital called Esperance.

With a bit of money coming in, Giles also joined the South Downs Gliding club near Glyndebourn

One day, after we had lived in Eastbourne for a year, and things had settled down nicely, Giles made a delivery of some pea shingle for a driveway to a large house in a nearby village called Hooe.

Looking down toward the end of the land, he saw an old garage or shed, and outside stood a blacksmith's anvil.

"What's that down there?" asked Giles.

"That's an old forge. It is part of the property."

Giles went to have a look and found a complete forge set up, including hearth, anvil and some tools. It wasn't in that bad a condition, and even had an electric blower to blow air onto the coals, rather than the bellows that he had to use as a boy.

Giles continued on his deliveries, but his mind kept coming back to the forge. Here was something that he could use and do. Maybe even make a living. After all, on his delivery rounds in the Sussex and Kent countryside, he passed house after house with stables and horses in the paddocks outside. They would all need a farrier.

The thought kept running around his head, and after a couple of days, he went back to the house and asked if he could rent the forge, and set up a smithy. A deal was struck, and Farrier Giles was born.

We all assumed that Giles business would take a little time to build, but it flourished very quickly. In fact all he had to do was shoe one horse and he was inundated with calls from all over asking for him to come and shoe for them.

There were two factors in this, the first was that there were literally hundreds of clients in the surrounding 30 miles. It was bucolic East Sussex and every village had a big house, whose owner had horses – so there was a big market. The second reason was that there was a dearth of decent farriers, in fact almost none. The vast majority of 'farriers' serving the area were not very well trained (if at all) and certainly not very qualified. Most weren't even farriers.

As soon as people learnt that there was a skilled, qualified farrier in the area, his books were full, as they left the cowboys, in droves, to become his clients.

As I remember, there was only one real farrier in the area who was competition for Giles. His name was Fred Gearing, and he was 84.

I met him whilst I was spending a day with Giles. He introduced me to this large, quiet spoken man with hands the size of plough shares.

"He's getting a bit old to do the job these days, and has help – from his brother. He's 82" said Giles.

At the end of his first year as a farrier, Giles business was booming, and he was a great success. Nothing could stop him now.

He applied to become part of the Worshipful Company of Farriers which is the guild for farriers formed in London in 1663.
After fulfilling all of the application requirements and tests, he
was admitted and awarded as a Member of the Worshipful Company of Farriers, with a certificate number of 360. That is only
the 360th person to receive the award since its inception, 310
years before.

Giles jokingly said he should put his prices up, and nobody made
a murmur. It was recognised that he was the best farrier in the
whole area, and his clients were mostly rich and could afford it.
He would charge £30 compared to competitors charging £15 for
a set of shoes.

Giles' client list included a sprinkling of Film and TV stars, like
Edward Woodward and Ronnie Corbett, and someone in their
family always had a horse.

A great many of his clients were very rich. Probably about 75%
of them were expat Londoners, who had moved out to the country. The husband would still commute, or possibly maintain an
apartment in Chelsea, as a pied-a-terre. They were often 'something in Banking' or 'the media' and their trophy wives had all
gone to Roedean.

The remainder were professional horse people, who bred,
trained, jumped, and evented horses.

Within 18 months of being a lorry driver, Giles was now part of
the 'horsey set'. He was on first name terms with David Broom,
Sir Godfrey Webster and Honor Blackman.

Giles was part of the horsey set, but sadly, it was as an onlooker
rather than as a member.

His rich clients didn't consider or treat him as a friend, and they didn't socialise with him. He was just another tradesman they employed. A valuable and important person to them, but a tradesman nevertheless. They were polite to him, but they weren't friends.

This really came home to him one day, when he arrived at a large manor house near Robertsbridge to shoe a couple of horses.

"Could you move your car round to the back of the house, by the servant's entrance?" he was asked by the client's wife.

At the front of the house were the owner's cars, 6 of them, each with ascending personalised number plates. His battered Citroen with 250,000 miles on the clock would look out of place.

It took some time, but he realised that his clients judged him on the car he drove, the job he did and the money he made, rather than for the person that he was.

Sometime in the 70's, Giles went off to a regimental reunion at Melton Mowbray. It had been more than 10 years since he had left the army and he looked forward seeing old friends.

After arriving, he spent a little time walking around the old buildings, reminding himself of his earlier life. He turned a corner, and saw a familiar figure; Sergeant Sandy Dixon.

Sandy stopped, and looked a Giles. After a second, he nodded, "Y'awl roight then, ba?" he asked.

"Foine, booiee," replied Giles. Sandy waved and moved off behind a stable.

Later that evening, at the dinner, Giles said, "I saw Sandy Dixon here."

"Oh, yes. He's still here."

"But he must be in his sixties," said Giles.

"Oh, we know. But nobody dares to tell Sandy he's too old, so he just continues working."

As far as I know, Sandy continued to work at Melton, but he may have moved to Speen (Horse Trust, army, Cavalry and Police horse retirement centre) under Brigadier John Spurry.

There was a higher standard of professional certification, which was to become a 'Fellow' of the Worshipful Company of Farriers. Giles accepted the challenge and over the next year, set about attaining this.

It required several exams and interviews, and would culminate with a highly specialised examination which would be held that year at Lord Vestey's estate in Gloucestershire.

I asked him who would judge him in his work and he said, "One of the other 5 or 6 people with this qualification, that are still alive."

Giles took the exams and passed. He became a 'Fellow' which is the highest standard of certification a farrier can achieve in Britain.

Interestingly, his exam coincided with the world shoeing championships, which were also being held at Vestey's estate at the same time.

"You should have a go at that," said a farrier.

And so, Giles entered the world shoeing championship, and he came third at his first attempt.

So Giles came back home with his bronze medal and his guild certificate, numbered 103. He was only the 103rd person to have this honour in 310 years. There were only about 5 people alive with this certification.

Given all of the publicity associated with this, Giles was offered two jobs; one to look after 250 polo ponies on a ranch in Argentina for a fabulously rich owner, and the other was as a Professor of Agricultural Studies at the University of Southern California.

He turned them both down.

"What!" shouted Liz. "You turned down Southern California!"

"I did it for you. I know that you don't like Americans," said Giles.

∞

Whilst in Gloucestershire, he was in the stables when three men came toward him. He thought that he recognised the middle one, but couldn't place him.

You know how it is, when you see someone and say, "I'm sure I know him from somewhere, but I can't put my finger on it."

"D'you think you might have a look at my pony?" he asked.

"No problem," Giles said and bent down to look at the horse's feet. It was at this moment he realised that the man he had recognised was Prince Charles.

"Bloody hell," thought Giles, and he got on with doing the work.

When he was finished, he handed the reins back to Charles.

"There you are. Good as new,"

Charles said "Must pay. How much?"

"50p?"

"Ah," said Charles patting his pockets, which were, as convention decreed, empty of money.

"No problems," said Giles, kneeling and patting his shoulder.

"Sorry, I'm not allowed to do that, and I don't have my sword with me," Charles said smiling.

"Can I put by Royal appointment on my van?"

"No, I just think my chaps will pay you the money," Charles said, pointing to one of his bodyguards to do the honours.

That evening, Giles went out to a local pub with a few of the other farriers and one of the bodyguards to celebrate his achievements.

The bodyguard was a big hit with the farriers.

"He's dead hard. He carries two bloody guns. Apparently if you grab him by one arm he will draw with the other and vice versa."

"He's a killing machine," said someone else.

"We should jump him just for fun," said a third, at the bar. "We won't hurt him. Just pin him down. Eh lads?" and he got nods of agreement from several, big, handy, strong and muscular Farriers.

"He won't be able to use kung fu when there's four of us sitting on his chest. When we get outside, we all jump him when I say 'moonlight'."

"Giles? You in?" they asked.

"No. It's not a good idea," he said.

And so the evening wore on with lots of beer and lots of laughs.

"What else have you done?" asked someone of the bodyguard.

"Before Royal protection, I was in Special services and Military intelligence."

"You must know Captain Brown," said Giles jokingly. And he

immediately regretted it, when he saw the bodyguard turn his head, pick him out, memorise his face and file it away for later review.

Giles knew that when he got back, the bodyguard would place a phone call to someone somewhere to ask for information of Giles Holtom, farrier, just to see if he was a threat or an asset.

"He said that he knew 'Captain Brown', sir which is an old code name, and he was with Prince Charles this afternoon," he would say.

"Balls," thought Giles. "Just what I need. A visit from Men in Grey Coats."

"'aven't you go 'omes to go to," said the barman, and they all finished off their pints and ambled outside to stand in the car park.

Giles stayed a bit behind the others.

"What do you think of the 'moonlight'?" asked a voice, and at the signal, they all jumped on the bodyguard.

The whole thing lasted less than 5 seconds, during which time he had broken one person's leg and another's arm before he controlled himself.

"We were only having a bit of fun," whined someone through a bloody and probably broken nose.

"Sorry," he said to the pile of bent and damaged farriers, and he wandered off down the lane, back to his lodgings at the estate.

"Told you," said Giles, handing one a handkerchief.

With his rise in popularity came an increase in invitations, and we were all invited to the annual Hunt Ball by the master of the hunt. Not only this, but we were placed on the whipper-in's table.

The whipper-in is in charge of the hounds and second in command to the Hunt master.

I duly went off to Moss Bros to rent a dinner suit for the evening, along with a pair of patent leather pumps to complete the ensemble.

We all drove to the Grand Hotel in Eastbourne (the only 5-star hotel for miles), and parked our car around the corner, away from the Mercedes and Rolls in the car park.

It was my first Ball, and something I had never seen before. The whole thing was a glittering, drunken affair filled with glittering, drunken people.

Once the dinner and speeches had finished, the night settled down to serious drinking and dancing. I approached the dance floor with great trepidation, which was justified when I fell on my backside, simply by standing on the polished dance floor. My patent leather shoes had soles with a mirror polish to match the uppers, and they had absolutely no grip whatsoever.

As I was gingerly picking myself up, a girl my age asked, "Who are you?"

"Mark. I'm the blacksmiths son," I replied.

"Oh," said Jacintha FFonts-Bittocks, looking me up and down. One of her friends giggled at me in my ill-fitting rented suit.

Jacintha evidently decided she would quite like a 'bit of rough', picked me up and pushed me onto the dance floor. It was here that I learned about my position in her society. I was a Grammar school boy, which basically meant I was an Oik, but at least not a dirty Oik from a secondary modern.

Her daddy owned a magazine, something like GQ. She had been sent to Roedean with a term in Switzerland for finishing. She had lots of money and now she was out to bring a title into the family.

She said that my social status meant that she would allow me to finger her behind the hotel, and If she liked me, she might give me a hand job. She only gave blow jobs to boys with a title, like Piers over there, and penetrative sex only after receiving an engagement ring. She appeared to have given it much thought and was quite strict about it.

I was Mellors to her Lady Chatterley and it was time to visit the potting shed.

We left at 1am, just before they all started racing silver tea trays down the main staircase and driving land rovers around the dance floor.

The drunken debauchery was allowed, nay, expected. It was the Hunt ball after all. The hunt would pick up the tab for the damages the next morning, and with thick heads, they would all meet and charge off in pursuit of some luckless fox.

The only problem with life, at this time, was Giles himself. He was still the same Giles that couldn't be bothered or motivated to get up and do his rounds as the Man from the Pru. In this case, he loved his work and enjoyed himself, but he was not interested in working too hard.

An energetic Farrier might shoe 8 horses in a day, or 3-5 if they were far away and required lots of travelling time. That would potentially put Giles on £200 a day and more, equating to anything from £20,000 to £50,000 in a year, which in those days, was a very, very healthy salary indeed. In fact he typically earned about £3,000 a year, which was a good, respectable income.

Giles could have earned ten times the income but he would have had to work ten times as hard. The opportunity was there but he couldn't be bothered to earn more. His day would consist of turning up to shoe one horse or maybe two, have a cup of tea and a chat, and keep on chatting until about 3pm and then come home.

Part of the problem was that Giles was not really interested in money. If he had it, he would spend it. If he didn't, then he wouldn't. It was as simple as that. But there was another part to this.

Giles never had any problem in getting other people to pay for him. He had no qualms about walking into a pub with no cash. Someone would always buy him a drink, and he was right, some-one usually would.

It was the same when people came to visit, we would go out to dinner and have a great party, but I never saw Giles pay the bill. It was always uncle Ted, or uncle Tom, or whoever had come to visit.

It wasn't that Giles was tight. He was free spending enough when he had money, but that wasn't often. Not nearly often enough.

I came home from school one day to find Giles had gone again.

"Where's dad?"

"He's in Hastings prison for a month for non-payment of his debts," said Liz.

I was sworn to secrecy, and told to make sure that nobody in the street knew about it. Dad was away for work somewhere. That was the story.

Another thing that I learned later in life was that Giles had been borrowing from the family, and relying on them to get him out of debt.

I believe that Granddad Rex had sorted out things in Yorkshire and that Granddad Bill had helped out when we were in East-bourne. Nothing was ever said, and no-one spoke about it, but

I do remember that Granddad Bill and Grandma Joan had cut him out of their wills, and left everything to Giles' sister, my auntie Jill. I believe they figured that they had already given him enough throughout their lives without leaving him any more.

We were the only people on our street who went abroad for their holidays. Admittedly it was camping, but it was in France. Everybody else went to Skegness or Blackpool.

Giles fitted out a small mini van, so that there were seats in the back and windows punched through the wall panels. The back was rammed with all our gear and off we went.

It should be remembered that Giles' grandparents were French and had forced him to speak French in the house, as a child. He rebelled and never spoke French again, which gave us a small problem when we pulled up at a petrol station on the first day.

"Mark," Giles said, pointing me out to the pump attendant.

Nobody had told me I was the official translator beforehand.

"Je, er. Je.." I blabbed. What was fill it up in French?

I thought of the literal translation and said, "Remplisser-ca, s'il vous plait."

"Fait le plein," replied the attendant, and he proceeded to put petrol into the car.

I was totally flummoxed and overjoyed.

I had actually spoken French, with an actual Frenchman. Not only this, but I had made a mistake, and it hadn't mattered. He hadn't laughed, nor had he pointed and scorned me. He had understood and had corrected me.

I was 14 and I could speak French.

Once this had happened, the flood gates opened and I couldn't stop speaking French at every opportunity. I avidly translated every sign, advert, and menu.

In the previous year at school, I had come 29th out of 31 in French. When I got back, I came second thereafter, and was only ever beaten by Peter Lambert, who was Swiss.

The only time I saw Giles speaking a foreign language was to bargain for a carpet in Arabic. This was top trumps, as most people spoke some level of French or German, but nobody spoke Arabic.

Three days from the end of that first holiday, Giles called a meeting.

"We have run out of money," he said. "I need all of your pocket money and holiday money to pay for petrol, so we can get home." And so we all put our money onto the table to pay for petrol.

The trip back was probably stressful for Giles and definitely for Liz, who couldn't stop moaning and complaining, but for the kids, it was exciting. Giles drove slowly up hills and coasted down them, to conserve petrol.

Just south of Paris, and with just one more day to go, Giles asked me to ask a local farmer if we could camp in his field (as we couldn't afford a campsite.

"Here looks good. Go ask him," and I did.

The farmer, Henri, welcomed us with open arms. He and his wife didn't speak a word of English, so I had to provide a running commentary.

"We could camp in that field, there," he said. He then invited all of the family to dinner with him that evening.

It turns out that Henri had 5 daughters and he confided in me that he spent his time as the only man sitting at his own dinner table surrounded by six women. He was overjoyed to be joined by a group of four males and only one woman. This would balance the situation.

In retrospect, the meal was one of the best we ever had, but at the time, it was full of stuff we had never had before.

We started off with an artichoke in front of each of us. We all looked at each other and nobody knew what to do with it, and so all eyes turned toward the end of the table, where Henri, with exaggerated movements, made a vinaigrette of wine and oil on his plate. He passed the ingredients down the table, and we all followed suit. Then he peeled off one of the artichoke leaves, dipped it into the vinaigrette and scraped the inner pulp off with his teeth.

"Was that it?" we all thought. Such a palaver for a tiny bit of sustenance.

The next course was pâté. Henri opened the grandfather clock, pulled out a long baguette, and began hacking pieces off that were passed down the table.

Again, nobody had ever eaten pâté before. This time I was less than happy as I had watched madame kill and prepare the rabbit earlier that afternoon. My squeamishness didn't stop anyone else, and the pâté was dispatched quickly.

After this we had a plate covered with a huge fish (I think a pike-perch) and green beans. The fish had come from Henri's pond and I fear it had suffered from the same fate as the rabbit.

By now, we had all had wine, and even Liz had warmed up. She and madame spoke, using me as interpreter.

At the same time, Giles was fast becoming best mates with Henri and was discussing farming and hunting, and they didn't seem to need me, even though neither spoke the other's language.

They decamped, with a bottle, into the lounge and started to listen to an LP of hunting horn music (really!). It seems that Henri was the Maître de la chasse and loved hunting wild boar in his forests.

On packing for the holiday, we had brought with us a selection of emergency food, just in case the French weren't civilised. This included tea bags, baked beans and an industrial 1kg jar of Maxwell house instant coffee. As we were leaving the next day, Liz offered the jar of coffee to madame, who it seems, loved Maxwell house.

In return, she offered to take us to visit her mother-in-law's chateau before we left. I checked before I translated.

"Chateau?" I asked.

"Oui."

And so we did.

The next day, Madame led the way on her Velosolex and we followed.

Sure enough, after a couple of miles, we arrived at a small chateau surrounded by a moat. The pastoral picture was made perfect by seeing the butler leaning out of the window with a rod, fishing for his tea.

Whilst Giles and Liz were being entertained, I was allowed to roam about the place, and found a 1916 Renault in chocolate and banana yellow. It looked as though the family had stopped using it because the ashtray was full.

Madame wanted a little help in fetching some water and so we set off into the woods with the car and a case of bottles to fill. The French do not trust their tap water, and only ever use it to bathe in or brush their teeth. We were invited to fill up our water bottles before we left. They obviously felt the same way about English water as well.

And so armed with some French spring water, we limped and coasted our way to the French coast and our ferry home.

We visited Henri and his family for the next 3 years, on the way back to the UK from the South of France. Each time he was happy to finally have as many men around the table as there were women.

I got home one day to find my mother in a foul mood.

"He's bloody gone again," she said.

This time it was permanent and they divorced.

It turned out that this time Giles had left Liz for another woman, Sue Haywood, who was one of his customers.

After the divorce, Giles married Sue, and they set about building a stud farm and horse centre. Sue provided the money, house and land, from her own divorce, whereas Giles provided the knowledge, skill and effort.

Sadly, this division of labour didn't work, and after only 6 months Giles and Sue divorced, with Sue keeping all of the property and equity. Giles was back on the street.

I don't really have a great deal to say about this, as I was 18 and had recently discovered girls, motorbikes and beer, so to be honest I wasn't really that bothered. By the time I was interested, it was already over.

Liz, on the other hand, took it very badly.

Her normal demeanour became more and more bitter. She took rejection very strongly, swinging from blazing anger to bouts of tears and recriminations. The worst part was that Liz simply stopped functioning as an adult.

She would go to work, would look after her patients, but on coming home, this stopped. She just didn't know how or refused to take responsibility for herself.

I remember her asking me to pay the gas bill, as she didn't know how to do it. She simply abdicated every decision to someone else – mostly me, and at 18, I was not really happy about becoming the 'man in the house' again.

This period lasted a few months, with Liz not going out and demanding that Van or I stay home with her. Then, but by bit, she got her confidence back and started to go back out into the world.

This was equally disconcerting, as more than once, I went to a club and came across Liz flirting and flaunting with some men. When your mum is the other side of the nightclub sitting on some guy's knee and kissing him, it is time to go.

The worst thing that happened in this period was me coming home after the pub and discovering Liz with some guy sitting in the front room watching a porno cine film being played on a bed sheet pinned onto the sitting room wall.

I was 18 and I really didn't want to be such a close spectator to my own mother's sex life.

After Giles' short lived second marriage, he moved to Battle and set up a forge there. Van had kept in contact and told me where he was, so I dropped by to see him.

He offered to take me out on a customer visit, so I hopped into his car, and off we went.

After 20 minutes driving through the deepest, darkest Sussex, we arrived at a large country estate house surrounded by acres of paddocks and woodland.

We got out by the stables and Giles set about looking at the horse. Soon we were joined by Mrs Ffont-Bittocks and her daughter Jacintha. Whether she recognised me, I don't know, but Jacintha just looked though me with cold, fish eyes. Apparently at the ball, I was a bit of rough, but here at her home, I was back to being an oik.

"Ah Giles," said Mrs Ffont-Bittocks, "The vet says he has a slight toe-in to his gait and suggest that you might make up some special shoes to correct him."

"Special shoes will cost quite a bit more," he replied.

"Oh, that's not a problem. I am sure your prices are very reasonable," said the woman whose husband's credit card paid for everything.

"It's important to fix him so we can improve Jacintha's riding results," she said over her shoulder, as they walked back to the main house.

"The damned horse is already better than the girl," Giles told me. "They buy a £5,000 horse for a £500 rider, and she won't ever get any better, but they think money will fix things. Anyway, she's 18 now, and will soon stop riding. She will want to swap it for a little MGB, and the horse will get sold. Just you wait and see."

This little exchange told me a lot about Giles' clients and what he thought about them. They were pleasant enough and provided income, but his passion and respect were for the 5% of clients that were proper, professional horse people.

On arriving back to the forge, Giles introduced me to his new girlfriend, Jenny.

She lived frugally in a small house in Battle. She didn't drive a car, but had a stable where she kept her horse, Wellington. She was definitely horsey set, but at the same time, not interested in position, image or money (or so it seemed).

I learned that, previously, she had worked in London in a high-powered job as a legal advocate for a theatrical production company. Her main job was to protect the company and to weed out plagiarism in the scripts submitted to them.

Even though she was a serious, Oxford educated, lawyer, she was also living in London in the swinging 60's as a dolly bird. She could enjoy, in equal parts, great freedoms and rampant sexism. She could go out and party with whomever she wanted, and was a high-level legal counsel, but she was still expected to get the boss a cup of tea when he wanted one.

In her everyday life, she would meet and consort with all of the writers and actors that came to the office. Given that the production company was very big and famous, so were the stars, and she ended up partying (and more) with many famous people of the time. This was a daily occurrence.

When I say, 'and more', Jenny admitted to having gone out with John Osbourne (Look Back in Anger), Richard Harris (A man Called Horse), and had even been instructed by her boss, Tony Beardsley, to take a bottle of whisky into an office where Sean Connery (James Bond) was waiting and not let him come out until he was ready to sign to do a film – whatever it took. Ah. The sacrifices she had to make for her job, being forced to sleep with

Sean Connery.

Anyway, for reasons best known to herself, she had given all of this up, and retired to the countryside to live a quiet and peaceful life with her horse.

Jenny seemed to be a woman of independent means. She was early forties, about the same age as Giles, but as far as I could see, she didn't have a job. Looking back, my guess is that she lived off the dividends from her share portfolio, as this seemed to be her only real financial asset.

Later on, I would learn that Jenny had quite a nice share portfolio, which I think, included shares in some of the company's productions, like Hair and Jesus Christ Superstar, so maybe she wasn't so badly off after all. At least, it seemed to be enough to retire on at the age of 45.

And along came Giles.

Every so often, Tony Beardsley would come down to visit Jenny. One time he came, ostensibly to ask her to come back to work for him in London, but in reality it was to show off his brand-new chestnut brown Rolls Royce.

He was in the middle of drinking a mug of tea (how quaint), when the phone rang and Giles was asked to go out to look at a horse.

"I'll be back in about an hour," he said.

"Can I come and watch?" asked Tony.

"Sure, but you'd better go in my car. It could be dirty."

"I have a better idea," said Tony. "I'll take you in my car. It would be fun to see their faces when you turn up in a Rolls."

They put Giles equipment into the boot and off they went.

Arriving at Sue Faulkner's yard caused quite a stir as Tony parked the gleaming Rolls in the middle of the stable yard.

"Follow my lead," said Tony, leaping out of the driver's seat and running round to open the door for Giles.

"Thank you Tony," said Giles. "Get out my stuff and put it over these please."

"Right away, Mr Holtom."

And Giles wandered off to inspect the horse as the rest of the yard gathered round to watch Giles' chauffeur take his equipment; a portable anvil, leather apron, hammers, tongs, files and assorted horseshoes, out of the boot of the Rolls Royce, and set them up in the corner.

Tony then doffed his cap to the assembled, and got back in the car to wait.

"What the hell have you been playing at?" demanded Sue Faulkner on the phone that evening.

"My phone has been ringing non-stop with people asking for the number of the new farrier I am using. It seems that he drives a Rolls Royce and has a chauffeur.

They figure if you can afford a Rolls then you must be the best, and they all want you to do their bloody horses too."

Despite the occasional fun and games, Giles (and Jenny) had fallen out of love with Sussex. The people judged you on how much you earned, and the car you drove, not on your character or capabilities.

More and more, each village was being filled with the village stockbroker, the village hedge fund manager, the village media tycoon and the village TV celebrity. There weren't any villagers left, and their houses had been combined, converted and updated. The village pub now had hanging baskets and sold Watney's red barrel and Chardonnay.

It was time for a move, and after a quick scan around they both agreed on moving to Wales.

18.   WE'LL KEEP A WELCOME IN THE HILLSIDE.

G iles' life so far had been one of lowly beginnings, in a small Essex village, with a steady rise in income, status and importance, until it reached its peak in Hong Kong.

The following years in Yorkshire marked a steady and prolonged decline and fall until the renewal he found in Eastbourne. But this was a false dawn. Whilst he was at least financially secure, he hadn't been happy.

Until now.

Giles and Jenny had bought a 20-acre, Welsh smallholding in Llanboidy. This was the start of the rest of their lives, and it was marked with contentment and satisfaction. It was the start of 30 years, being happily not-married.

∞

Giles had gone down to the house a week early to get things habitable, whilst Jenny closed up and sold everything in Battle.

As he arrived at the farm house he found 6 eggs, a loaf of bread, some butter and a pint of milk on the doorstep. There was no note.

He didn't know anyone in the area, and couldn't understand how anyone even knew he was coming, and yet here on the doorstep was a welcome.

"It can't have been Mrs Ffont-Bittocks.," thought Giles. "She would never have thought of this, and if she did, they would have been quail's eggs."

The nearest house was a mile away and there wasn't a soul in sight to see Giles grateful smile and quick jig of happiness.

Wales was everything the Giles and Jenny wanted. It was like his Essex childhood. Most people didn't have much, and what they had, they willingly shared. Barter was a common currency.

Wales can be a very welcoming or a very hostile place, depending upon who you are.

If you bought the nice little cottage so you could come down for the weekend to decompress and get away from London, then people hated you. It was very common for folk to shun incomers like this, often refusing to speak to them.

"Sorry. I haven't the English, Bach," they might say. "Siarad Cymraeg, ti Saesneg pigog." Which meant "Speak Welsh, you English prick?"

On the other hand, if you integrated and provided something of value to the community, then you were willingly accepted.

"What do you do, Bach?"

"I'm a farrier," said Giles.

"Welcome. Welcome, Bach."

Had he said, "I'm a hedge fund manager," they would have responded with, "Ti Saesneg pigog," but a farrier would do very nicely, thank you.

Giles fitted into Welsh life perfectly. It was a society based on community, sharing and caring, rather than individualism, exploitation and profit.

But for Giles, the main thing was barter.

Anywhere you go in the UK, you expect to pay for what you buy. But not necessarily in Wales. Here they often used a system of barter, exchanging goods or effort for other goods.

It was perfectly common for Giles to do welding for someone and to be paid in eggs, or lamb. Both parties were happy, and most important of all, no money had changed hands, so there was no tax liability. Giles, like many country people, had a phobia of paying too much tax, or in fact any tax at all.

Soon he was part of the barter economy, and had agreements to shoe people's horses in exchange for them cutting and baling his hay, and many similar arrangements.

The other thing to understand about Wales is that the normal laws of Geography and Physics don't hold true. Specifically when you want to get somewhere.

If you want to go to town from the house, the drive is uphill, and yet for some reason that only applies in Wales, the drive from town back home is also uphill.

In fact the only true statement you can make about travel in Wales is that, to get anywhere from anywhere, you have to go uphill.

The final thing to know about Wales was that people always had a hobble.

I asked Giles what a hobble was, and he explained it was partly a hobby and partly a second job, and often one that provided income which was not necessarily declared.

So, I learned that the local postman was also the egg man, and that he delivered (his own hen's) eggs on his postal rounds.

I was surprised to be told to go the grocer, when I asked where I could buy a bottle of wine, until I learned that the grocers was also an unlicensed off-license.

I imagine that the butcher was also a baker and candlestick maker, thus making it simpler to cast for TV versions of children's rhymes.

◆ ◆ ◆

Giles hobble was sheep. He and Jenny bought a flock of 80 Llanwenog sheep and a sheep dog, Jack, which came with the flock. The sheep were a rare breed and within a year Giles had become the President of the Llanwenog sheep society.

Jack was a proper 'one man and his dog' sheep dog, and could be controlled with whistles and cries of "come by" and other country shouts and noises. Given that Giles only had 20 acres and their sheep came, like pets, when they were called, this was a skill that was not really needed.

To them, Jack was just a pet, but to others he was a valuable commodity, and shepherds would often come round and ask Giles if they could borrow Jack for a day to bring the sheep in from the hills.

Jack loved doing this, and in the system of barter, Giles and Jenny would receive something in return, like a chicken or maybe some cuts of lamb for the freezer.

On the day of the local county show, one man came round and asked to borrow Jack. He wanted to enter the sheepdog trials and jack was a highly trained, expert dog.

Sheepdog trials are basically a display of skill and control between a shepherd and his dog, and their ability to manoeuvre a flock of 6 sheep through and around obstacles on a course set out on a hillside.

The shepherd must use the dog to gather the sheep, move them from one place to another, perhaps through a gate, then back around the field following a specific path, and finally to put them all together in a small sheep pen constructed of wooden stiles with a gate.

Jack, being a highly trained sheep dog was a very valuable asset, and the guy was likely to win a prize for the trial.

All started perfectly, and continued in the same way.

The shepherd stood in the centre of the field and, using Jack, brought the sheep safely through the gates and around the obstacles. All that was left was putting them into the pen.

To do this, he placed himself between the sheep and the pen and slowly reached for the gate with his shepherd's crook. He hooked and opened it very slowly, very steadily, so as not to start the sheep. He gradually opened the gate and when it was wide enough he turned round, but, to his surprise, the field was empty. There was no Jack and no sheep.

Of course, he was the only one who didn't know this. When he was busy concentrating on opening the gate, the crowd had watched enthralled, as Jack get bored of waiting and decided to herd the sheep into another pen elsewhere.

Jack took them, all together, off the field and headed toward the beer tent. The occupants, quietly having a pint were disturbed by 6 sheep milling around the bar.

The crowd thought that this was excellent entertainment, and sat and watched as on the one hand the shepherd was slowly opening a pen with no sheep behind him, and on the other people were busy throwing sheep out of the beer tent only to have them herded back in by Jack.

"Best sheep trial ever," they said.

I went down to visit Giles and Jenny.

"We can eat out. My treat," I said.

I learned that the nearest restaurant was more than 15 miles away (uphill), but that we would get Chinese take away which was in town only 5 miles away. As I was living in London, with 2 takeaway shops on my street and 5 restaurants withing 10 minutes stroll, I found this isolation hard to understand.

"Never mind," said Giles, sensing my disorientation. "I'll take you to the local pub afterwards. You'll enjoy it." And so off we went.

I wasn't really expecting someone's front room, but that is exactly what it looked like. I had been in lots of old pubs, in and around London. They had horse brasses on the wall, hanging baskets by the door, oak beams, subdued lights in sconces and a roaring fire.

As we walked in, everybody was speaking Welsh, but on seeing Giles, they switched to English out of friendship and respect. I guess that if it had just been me, they would have continued in Welsh.

This place had a mix of Formica and wooden tables. No two chairs were the same. The lights were harsh fluorescent tubes, the floor was lino and there was no bar. Where did you get the beer and what beer did they serve?

"Have a seat," said Giles. "I will be back a minute." And he took off to chat with someone on the other side of the room.

After 30 seconds a man emerged from what looked like a larder, carrying a large enamel milk jug. He walked up to the table, deposited a pint glass in front me and filled it from the milk jug, which was full of beer that he had poured fresh from the barrel in the larder.

This was definitely not a place to ask for a pint of lager, or a gin and tonic for that matter. As far as I could see, they had one beer and a couple of bottles of spirits. Given that many people in Wales were Chapel, at lot of the women would be drinking lemonade or cups of tea.

"Thank you," I said, looking around. I saw an older guy sitting on the settle a couple of feet from me and said, "The beer looks good."

"Pardon?"

"I said, the beer looks good."

"Yes."

"Do you live locally?" I asked.

"Pardon?"

I said, do you live locally."

"Yes."

At this moment Giles came back to the table and nodded to the old guy.

"I wouldn't bother speaking to Bryn," said Giles.

"Why?"

"He only knows two words in English. 'Pardon' and 'Yes'.

But he is a very interesting man. His job is maintaining the A40 through this part of the county, and his best mate is the Local Lord.

You see, people here are friends because of who you are, not what you are. That's the real reason we left Sussex and came here."

I looked around the pub at the locals, sitting under the harsh light. It was dowdy, charmless, and totally unattractive, but the beer was good, and somehow this 'front room' in the middle of nowhere looked better and more welcoming than any beautiful, antique filled, bijou, historical haunt in Chalfont St. Giles.

I mentioned this to Giles, who looked at me and said, "It's not the same since they modernised it."

"Modernised! How?"

"They have an indoor toilet now."

Apparently, before this plumbing revolution came to Llanboidy, people used to just walk across the road and pee into the field opposite.

"What about the women?"

"Oh, they all used to go at once. One would stand guard at the door, so no man could leave and the others would go into the field together."

I looked around the room, noticing the women sat chatting in groups, drinking mugs of tea, separate from their men, who were gathered on different tables smoking around overflowing ashtrays.

Giles was right. It probably was better before modernisation, and I was glad to see it before it disappeared completely.

Giles and Jenny lived in Llanboidy for 5 glorious years, but then decided to move on, and looked to find something better for horses. They settled on Llandeilo which was a small town near Carmarthen.

The house itself was 20 acres situated about 10 miles from town, so it was still miles from anywhere.

I was visiting Giles once, and we were on our way to look at some animals in Tepee valley when he told me the story about the "man who didn't exist".

Apparently, a family had a child, who in those days, was called 'slow'. He was not on the spectrum, nor was he deformed. He simply had a mental age of a boy of 8.

Given the way the community worked, if there was ever problem, for example if he wandered off, someone would take him in, give him a cup of tea and take him home.

He was known, supported and loved by the community.

And then his parents died and he was alone.

Well the community continued looking after him. Taking it in turns to house and feed him. In return he would feed the chickens or muck out the pigs.

When he got a little older, say in his late teens, he didn't like to stay in houses, and would walk off into the hills and woods and stay outside. Coming back down into the valley when he was hungry.

And this went on for a long time.

It got into a routine where (let's call him) Dylan would turn up one night and sneak into a barn to get warm. If the owner saw him in the morning, Dylan would offer to do some chores in exchange for a little food. He might stay in the barn for a week or a month, and then one day he would be gone, only to pop up at a different farm further up the valley.

Over the years, Dylan became more and more feral. He spoke less and less, and then only Welsh. He wouldn't come indoors.

The women would find him an old pair of trousers or a coat from their husband and give them to him. Perhaps an old pair of shoes or wellingtons if they could get the right size.

By the time Giles told me about 'Dylan', he was in his sixties. He was an old ghost/man who wandered around the woods, fixing fences, before the farmer had noticed they were knocked down.

"But he's so old. Why doesn't someone help him?" I asked.

"He doesn't exist," replied Giles.

"He has never been registered born, nor been to school. He has no National Insurance number, has never earned anything and never paid tax. He will not get a pension. He is not in any computer anywhere. Apart from the few people in this and the neighbouring valleys that know him, he doesn't exist."

Of course, there are stories of men who have lived alone for years on remote desert islands, like Robinson Crusoe. But I would never have believed there was one living in the fields and valleys around Giles' house.

Tepee valley is a place about 20 miles from Giles, where a commune of hippies lived. They lived off the land, growing their own food, etc.

Their place was a few acres at the end of a valley where they had constructed a few shacks, sheds, tents and yurts.

The locals called it Tepee valley.

"I should warn you," said Giles, as we turned into the valley, "they are naturists, and like to walk around naked. I didn't want you to stare. You get used to it."

Well we duly arrived, with me prepared. To be honest, it would not be a problem. I had studied at theatre school and was used to sitting in a dressing room full of naked and semi-naked actors wandering around putting on make-up. This couldn't be any weirder than that.

And yet it was.

I got out of the car to find that everybody was wearing clothes. Well, at least they were all wearing hand knitted sweaters - but nothing else.

It seems that the Welsh climate is not very conducive to naturism, so the hippies made themselves nice, warm, hand knitted jumpers to keep their core body warm, but for some reason, they didn't feel the need to make them longer than waist length.

So I was faced with groups of people of both sexes wandering by in sweaters, but with their kit dangling out on display.

"I can get very off putting if they stand too close while I am trimming their donkey's hooves," said Giles.

Giles and Jenny lived like this for the next 20 years. Life was good, simple and uncomplicated, and then one day, when Giles was about 65, he bought a computer.

Up until then, he had written the newsletter of the Llanwenog sheep society by hand, and Jenny, worked part time for the National Trust, would word process and then photocopy it.

Now He had a computer, he could do all of this himself, and within a short time, he was also emailing the newsletter to the members.

Over the next few years, Giles started using the computer more and more. He discovered the internet, and bulletin boards. Here he could find and participate in discussions on sheep and even farriery.

Giles was fascinated by the capabilities and information available to him in this brave new world. So much so, that he wanted to know more, so at the ripe old age of 69 he enrolled in a computer programming course, and over the next months, built his own website and blog.

@FarrierGiles was on the internet, and amongst those that are interested in such things, he became quite a celebrity, regularly hosting web meetings to discuss aspects of farriery.

And then, one day around 2006 @FarrierGiles received an email request, to ask if he would judge at the upcoming shoeing championships, to be held in Austin, Texas.

Giles explained that he would love to, but he had to arrange for someone to look after the animals, and there was the question of costs for planes, etc.

"No problem," came the reply. They offered return tickets for both Giles and Jenny, and a paid hotel reservation for the duration of their stay. They were also proposing to pay him $1,500 for his services as a judge. "Would this be acceptable?"

"Where do I sign?" said Giles, and off they went to Texas.

Being Americans, they did things in a much bigger and better way than the UK. Part of this was the hoopla they raised around Giles, and he found himself in the centre of a media bubble, as "The world famous @FarrierGiles".

I think his proudest moment was seeing people walking around the show wearing "I've been judged by @FarrierGiles" T-shirts.

At the end of the show, the organisers took Jenny and him to a famous restaurant, The Cattleman's Club, where they informed Giles, he would have the best steak in the whole world.

"How would you like your steak, sir?" asked the waitress.

"Medium rare, please."

"And your vegetable? We have Mashed potatoes, French fries, home fries, steak fries, jacket potato or hash browns." Giles was a bit nonplussed by the idea that the only vegetable available was potatoes, 6 different ways.

And then the steak arrived. Well, if by best they meant biggest, they were certainly correct, as he was presented with a steak that weighed 1kg (2lbs).

The meal concluded, they organisers then presented Giles with Silver belt buckle. This being Texas it was the size of a small plate, and it was engraved with the championships and his name.

Then, over the coffee and brandies, someone asked Giles about his career and how he had become a farrier.

"Well," said Giles, and so he started to tell his stories.

The Americans were enthralled, and ensured him that he needed to write down these stories in a book, better still, a film.

A reporter writing up the show for a magazine, gave Giles his card, "We should keep in touch. Maybe we can do something with these stories," he said.

Well, neither Hollywood, nor the reporter got back to him, so this part has now been left to me.

At age 75, four things happened for Giles; he had a minor heart attack, he went back to school, he celebrated 30 years not being married to Jenny and he was co-opted onto a government study group.

The heart attack was actually angina, and the doctor stressed to Giles that this was a warning from his body and he should listen to it, and take note.

He was told to give up smoking and to stop working. And so, after having smoked a pack a day for the previous 60 years, Giles gave up smoking. Instead of getting better his health gradually deteriorated and he gained 30kg (60lbs) in weight and developed late-onset Diabetes type 2 – but he never smoked again.

As for his education, in a chance discussion with a neighbour, it was suggested that Giles might enrol at the University of Wales, to study for a PhD on aspects of farriery. Given that his only education to date was that he had matriculated and left school at 16, this sounded both interesting and daunting, but after meeting with a university mentor, he was persuaded that this was something that he might do.

And he did, graduating around 2005 as Doctor Giles Holtom PhD.

Giles invites us all down to celebrate not being married to Jenny for 30 years. He had booked out a pub owned by the National Trust, called Mein Clwyd, which was a few miles from their home.

It was a great day, with all of their friends gathered together and milling around.

I was sitting in outside in the sunshine when a little old lady walked up to me. She looked like a cross between a Velociraptor and a budgerigar.

"Your father won't get any of my money. Nor any of you. I'll make sure of that," she hissed at me.

"It was a pleasure to meet you too," I replied, moving off before her budgie-raptor claws tried to dig into my skin.

"Who is that old woman over there?" I asked Giles.

"Jenny's mother," he replied. "We don't get on."

That was the only time I ever met Jenny's mother, and the only thing she ever said to me.

Well, I can now report that the old bat was right. I never saw a penny of her money. Neither, I believe, did Giles. It's a good job. I didn't want it in the first place.

I have no knowledge why, but perhaps because of the minor stir from Giles' Doctorate, he was invited to sit on a government committee to discuss and advise the (Blair) government on maintaining and safeguarding UK country pursuits, skills and traditions.

I knew about this, because Giles would drive down to the meetings in London, and use the opportunity to break his journey and stay the night at my house on the way back to Wales.

"So, what were you doing in London?" I asked.

"Oh. I'm part of a government committee on the countryside. They seem to think I will be useful as I am a farrier."

"Wow, so you are advising the government. Who's on the committee?"

"The majority of people on the committee are MPs who live in places like Surbiton. Then it's just me and Princess Anne."

"What! You are on a committee with Princess Anne?"

"Oh yes. We get on very well actually. They place her at the head of the table next to the chairman, but she always moves her stuff and comes to sit next to me, saying, "I hope you don't mind, but I prefer to sit next to my friend, Giles". Then she spends most of the meeting whispering to me and telling dirty jokes. The chairman doesn't like it, but there's not much he can do about it."

"How come she likes you?"

"I think it's because I'm the only one who actually lives in the country and continues the traditional ways, at least with horses. You know she is a horsey person, so we get on well."

One time, Giles came down to London by train and after his trip, I offered to drive him back to Wales.

After driving about 50 miles along the M4 Giles told me to slow down and pull over onto the hard shoulder.

"Are you OK?" I asked.

"Just drive to that gate over there," He instructed.

"This isn't an exit. The slip road is 5 miles from here." Nevertheless I did as he asked. We drove up to a large electric gate with a camera and speaker by the gatepost.

"Push the button," Giles said and then leaned over and talked into the speaker.

"Giles Holtom," he said, and the gates buzzed and opened.

I drove though and then followed a track over a couple of fields until I could see a stable block in the distance, which was where we were headed.

"Don't go too far from the car. They don't like it," said Giles, pointing at the security cameras, and he wandered off into the stables.

I waited by the car for 20 minutes, occasionally seeing Giles emerge from one stable and then disappear into another. As far as I could see, there was no-one else around. The place was eerily quiet, with the silence only broken by the occasional snort or hoof stamp from a horse.

I walked to the end of the stable block to see what was behind and was surprised to see a swimming pool, just as Giles appeared at my shoulder.

"They treat the stable boys well here. They even have a pool," I noted.

"That's for the horses. Physiotherapy," said Giles. "Come on. Let's go. I've done here."

And so I drove out through the stables across another couple of fields to arrive at another automatic gate giving onto a small country road. The gate whirred open as I drove up.

"What was all that about?" I asked.

"Those are some of Sheik Ali Maktoum's horses. He has asked me to check on them every time I go past, and to write a report outlining any problems I find and remediation I recommend. I send the report by email and he sends me a cheque."

"Wow," I thought. Princess Anne and Sheik Ali Maktoum all in one day.

19.   FINAL CURTAIN

That is pretty much all of the stories.

Giles died in his sleep a couple of years later, 2 weeks before his 83rd birthday.

In my opinion, everybody's life turns on small incidents. Often these are not even recognised as key until way after the fact.

If only I had married her.

If only I had taken that job.

If only I hadn't gone out that night, etc.

I believe, for Giles, these key points were when his father refused to allow him to stay in education, when the army needed farriers, and when he got off the train in Yugoslavia. All contributed to Giles living in places and through amazing adventures that are just not possible in today's world.

These points caused his life to shoot up like a firework. He had a good career, money, a rich life, a pretty wife, kids.

And then the next key point, when Liz decided that she wanted Giles to leave the army rather than re-enlist. From this time we see a decline and fall, leading to failure, unhappiness, bankruptcy, poverty, abandonment, divorce and even jail.

Then, just when things couldn't get any worse, Giles saw the anvil outside a disused forge and his life as a farrier began.

As a farrier, Giles finally became what he was meant to be. This change stabilised and dragged Giles back from the previous lows not to new heights but to contentment and happiness, that was to last until the end of his life.

At the start, I asked you to visualise Giles ambling, like a country boy, and that's what he did. He ambled through his life.

Other people are driven through their life by ambition and money, but not Giles. He was the least ambitious person I ever met.

On the other hand, Liz's ambition for Giles was very apparent. She wanted him to look for promotion, to move up in the army, and she was disappointed in him when, in Germany, he turned down the opportunity to move out of the ranks and go to the Officer Training Course.

Liz desperately wanted to be a Captain's wife, or even a lieutenant, whereas Giles already knew that Captains were actually largely administrative figures. They didn't do veterinary work, or shoe horses, they arranged the running of the corps, ordered supplies, assigned postings and looked after paperwork (at least that's what he thought), and he definitely didn't want to do that. He was happy being a vet, a dog trainer and a farrier.

Later, when Giles moved into civilian life, Liz's ambition was for him to be a 'manager'. He could start as the Man from the Pru, but after a few years he could be promoted to looking after all Dewsbury, and then later maybe even West Yorkshire! By the time he was 50, he could apply to be an alderman for the council and she would get a new wool coat with a real fur collar. She had it all mapped out.

This was her dream. It wasn't Giles'. He dreaded waking up and going to work. He didn't want to be a manager. He didn't want to do paperwork. He was not interested in status, which was so important to Liz, and this of course, is where things went wrong.

The funny thing was, when Giles came across the anvil and then decided to become a farrier, he actually did discover an ambition, and a strong one. He wanted to be the best Farrier he could be, maybe the best in the world. But he would do it his own way, by ambling toward it. Not too fast and not too slow, with his feet at 10 to 2.

◆ ◆ ◆

There is one final thing.

It was 3.00am and Giles and I were sitting around my kitchen table drinking white wine.

I had a pad in front of me covered with scribbles and notes. I had patched together a likely timeline of Giles' travels and had checked the background to several of his stories.

I realised that there was one question that I hadn't asked Giles. One that hadn't been answered for over 45 years, and if I didn't ask it now, I probably never would.

I took a deep breath and said, "Why did you leave us when I was a kid?"

He thought about this for a moment, deciding whether to respond, and then he said, "Liz was having an affair."

For 45 years, I had heard the arguments and statements made by Liz and her mother, that Giles was a bastard, a man who had run out on his kids, a good-for-nothing who didn't care about us.

That was true wasn't it? What if it wasn't? What if Giles was right? My world started to crumble before my eyes.

My brain was whirling with questions and snap shot views of my early life played in front of my eyes. "He's a lazy bastard. He's a liar." Then I saw Liz sitting in the front room watching porn with some guy who was hoping for a shag.

I was gobsmacked. In just a few seconds I had to re-evaluate my whole opinion of the man. What if he wasn't a bastard?

"Who was it?" I asked.

"I don't wish to speak ill of the dead and you don't need to know. It's not important."

So there it was. I had started with the simple intention of writing my father's stories. Maybe find out a little more about him on the way, and finally, after all of this chatting, I had finally found an answer to a question that I have had since I was 10 years old.

PART III: IT'S NOT ME. IT'S MY FAMILY.

F inally, because they are so outlandishly unreal, I have added several other Holtom stories, just to show it is a family trait, rather than just Giles.

20. LARRY THE LAMB

Larry was my third granddad. Yes I had three. He met my grandmother, Hilda, when she was married to Bill during the war.

Larry was desperately in love, but refused to have anything to do with Hilda until she was formally divorced. This happened when it could be sorted out, after Bill and Larry came back from the war, so they got married in April 1947.

I got married in March 1997 and was going down to visit Larry and Hilda, when she died, just 2 weeks before their 50th anniversary.

I have never known a man so in love as Larry was with Hilda. I learned that they had only spent a total of 10 days apart in their 49 years, 11 months and 2 weeks together. Larry was totally and completely bereft.

I wanted him to move to a home a couple of miles from us instead of the drive, 110 miles each way, I made to see him, but he didn't want to move far away from Hilda, and so I did the commute.

Larry was staying with us for the weekend, and I asked if he wanted to go to the cinema with us. We were going to see "Saving Private Ryan".

"What did you think of that?" I asked.

"Ay. It were like that," Larry replied.

"I beg your pardon. How would you know?"

"I was there."

Before I tell you this, I need to explain that Larry was a small, 5 foot, 5 inch (165cm), mild mannered, Yorkshire tailor, who loved ballroom dancing. He was the single most inoffensive man I have ever met.

"What do you mean you were there? Do you mean D-day?"

"Ay. Royal Artillery. We landed after the infantry had established a beach head and provided artillery support for them moving forward."

"Bloody Hell," I thought. I would never have considered Larry as a soldier, never mind part of the D-Day landings.

"What was it like?"

"It were like it were in't film. Bullets whizzing over your head and ricocheting off the tanks and guns.

We had to provide artillery support for the infantry, who were in front of us. Once secured, we would advance by moving through and leap-frogging the infantry/.. Then they would leap-frog us.

One time the Germans counterattacked before the infantry came and we were the front line. They were 100 yards in front of us, across the other side of a field, and they were so close we couldn't depress the guns to shoot them, so we had to use rifles.

My mate Chalky and I hid behind a sand bag, shooting at them.

The Germans started to come across the field toward us and the sergeant called for rapid fire, and we all shot as fast as we could. I remember Chalky going 'Oooh' as we were shooting. The Germans ran back to the hedge and disappeared.

We had to wait 10 minutes like that and then all of a sudden, the infantry walked through us and moved the line forward.

It was then that I looked at Chalky and saw that he was dead, lying next to me.

I remember that his wife had just sent him a parcel, so it was my job as his mate, to write to his wife and tell her. She had sent him a cake, which we all shared."

I could see the glint of a tear in Larry's eye as he told me and remembered his pal. Maybe in mine too.

"So where else were you in the war?" I asked.

"Oh, Battle of the Bulge, Arnhem, fight across the Rhine. All over really. The worst was relieving Belsen."

"You were at Belsen? Wow. What was that like?" I asked.

"I don't want to talk about it, or even think about it. I still have nightmares sometimes." And Larry refused to talk to me any more about the war.

I did some research, and it is true that Belsen was liberated by a corps of the Royal Artillery. The German guards had run away just a couple of days before, leaving over 13,000 bodies lying stacked like wood, around the compound. Anne Frank had died there just 2 weeks before and when Larry arrived there were over 60,000 Jews starving to death in front of his eyes.

Over the next few weeks the inmates continued to die at an alarming rate, as they were so starved that giving them normal food simply put their bodies into shock and they died anyway.

The captain commanding the unit was so incensed by what he saw, that he forced every single member of the nearby village to walk through the camp to see what had been done, but which they said they were unaware of, being 3 miles away. He made sure that they looked at the prisoners and the corpses rather than look away or at the ground.

In civilian life, Larry went back to being a tailor in the winter and running a boarding house in Southport during the summer, which is where Giles met Liz whilst he was on leave.

21. THE 13TH HOLE.

The best way to describe Giles' dad, Bill, was to say that instead of waiting for his ship to come in, like most people, he swam out to find it.

All through his life, money had been scarce, and Bill had become adept at finding situations and making deals that were profitable to him. It was never easy, but Bill almost always came out in front.

After the war he started a new business. He knew all of the local farmers, and the cars that had been laid up during the war, either to avoid being commandeered for the War effort, or because the owner couldn't get the petrol coupons.

He would do up the old cars, get them running and sell them on (for a profit).

One vehicle he couldn't sell on was a 1928 Morris 30 cwt van. Never mind. It worked, and he would find a use for it one day.

The day came soon after, when a farmer asked if Bill could pick up and deliver ½ ton of potatoes, which he did (for a price).

"I hear you're going to get some potatoes from Pearson's. Can you pick me up a hundredweight?" asked a friend in the village.

"If you're going, can you get me half a sack as well?" asked another.

And so Bill's grocery business was born.

He would travel round the farms, picking up produce and delivering back into town, where an eager populace was waiting to buy from him.

Bill spotted an opportunity, and this carried on for a couple of months. Then he bought a small house in the centre of Halstead. He knocked out the front wall and window and replaced it with a shop front. He had made his first Grocer's shop.

Bill wasn't really interested in sitting in a shop selling carrots all day. He preferred doing the driving and picking up the produce, so he hired a man to look after the shop, and rented him the rooms upstairs to live in as part of his salary.

By the time Bill retired, he owned three Spar supermarkets.

∞

When Bill 'retired', he didn't actually want to, but Joan forced him to do it.

"We have enough money. Just take it easy and go and take up golf," she told him.

Bill didn't know how to play golf, and so took an evening class in the local school where they taught him how to hold the club, the stance and swing.

After a couple of months, they professed that he was ready to actually go and play, so Bill went to the local golf course and asked to play a round.

"You have to be a member, Sir."

"OK. Then make me a member," replied Bill.

"You have to be proposed and seconded," he was told. "And then, there are the fees."

"How much is that?" Bill asked, and they told him.

"Kerrist! That's a working man's wage!"

And so, Bill didn't become a member of the Essex Golf and Country Club.

But he wasn't going to waste 2 months of hitting a ball against a wall at the school, and certainly not to be beaten by those toffee-nosed twerps.

If the bastards wouldn't let him play, he would build his own golf course. So Bill hopped in his car and drove off to see an old friend of his, who sold him a couple of fields.

And without ever having played a round, Bill built a golf course.

Bill was happy, because he had something to do, rather than 'retire'.

He laid out the course, landscaped the holes, removed trees, dug bunkers, and made fairways and greens.

Things went really well. In fact, all was perfect, until one day, when the course was built and Bill was finishing off the landscaping, when someone told him that there was no such thing as a 13-hole golf course.

"How am I supposed to know that?" said Bill. "I haven't even played a game yet." And so he went back to his friend and bought another field off him to develop another five holes.

When the course was finished, Bill played it several times, even getting quite good, but after a few short months, he became bored with golf. He preferred driving the Ransome's mower flat out, up and down the fairways, seeing if he could beat his time for cutting the grass.

Bill looked around for other things to do, and then the doorbell rang.

It was a man who asked if Bill owned the warehouse and factory unit in Halstead, which he did. He had taken it in payment for a debt, thinking he would find a use for the factory sometime, and that it would be worth keeping. Well, now was that time.

"Can I use the machinery that has been left in the factory? It's specialised equipment that we need for our process. We will pay you for it."

Bill agreed, but then found out that payment might be difficult, as they were a start-up company with very little cash.

"What if we gave you 20% of our company, in lieu of the rental and machinery hire?" they asked, and Bill agreed. He now owned 20% of Halstead carpets.

What Bill learned was that Halstead carpets had just invented a new, rubber backed carpet tile. The tiles used pig bristle instead of wool and they were incredibly hard wearing. They could be dyed in any colour and were perfect for high traffic areas, in offices and shops. In fact in any area where people wanted carpet instead of a concrete floor.

"They sound good," said Bill. "How are you going to sell them?"

"We are sending samples all over the country to companies that build offices. If they like them, they can specify them as part of the build."

"That sounds great. But that means you have to have someone driving samples all over the place, instead of making product. What you need is a driver – and I just happen to have a bit of time on my hands."

And so Bill became the unofficial delivery driver for Halstead carpets.

Every day, Bill would get up, and after breakfast, would put his golf clubs into his car, kiss Joan, and set off to play a round. He didn't want Joan knowing that he was working again.

Then, he would drive to the factory to see if they had and samples to deliver. If not, then he would continue to the golf course, but if there was a delivery, he would throw it in the back of the car and drive it to the new customer.

Sometimes the delivery was local, in Essex, and other times it was elsewhere in the country, like Glasgow. These were the days before overnight couriers, and the only way to get a parcel to Glasgow quickly was to send it by Red Star on the train from Kings Cross in London, so Bill would drive down to London for the day.

◆ ◆ ◆

Then one day, "We've got an important order, Bill. But it has to go to Sweden. We have worked it out and arranged that, if you can get it onto this ship, they will take it for us."

"OK. Where is the ship?"

"Newcastle."

Newcastle was 300 miles away and the drive would take 5 hours, each way.

"Hmmm. This will take some thinking," said Bill, who didn't want Joan to know that he wasn't playing golf, but how was he going to stay away for more than 10 hours?

He went home, rushed in and kissed Joan.

"What are you doing home? Is golf cancelled?"

"No darling. I just got to thinking, how I never make enough of a fuss of you."

"What?"

"Yes. I thought it might be nice to just pack a bag, jump in the car and drive. It would be like a mini honeymoon," he said.

"Oh, Bill," Joan cooed.

"Enough of that,. Hop upstairs and pack an overnight bag. Let's go."

"Where shall we go?" asked Joan.

"I don't know," said Bill. "I just feel like driving. Let's see where we end up."

And so they set off.

After an hour of driving, Joan looked out of the window and said, "Here looks very nice. We could stop at that pretty looking pub."

"No. Let's keep going."

After another hour, the same thing happened, and then again after 3 hours. By the fourth hour, they had gone past Scarborough. Robin Hood's bay and the North Yorkshire moors. Joan had fallen silent.

Just after 3pm, the arrived in the outskirts of Newcastle, which is a town built on mining, ship building and fishing. It was grim, black and heavily industrialised. Joan was still silent.

Bill followed the signs and headed for the port. Arriving, he drove up to the entrance barrier and wound down the window.

"Pier 14, The Vasteras?"

"Down there, second on the left."

Bill drove to the pier, got the parcel out of the boot, and ran up the gangplank.

He came back down and got into the car.

"This looks like a nice place," he said, ignoring the docks, cranes, and ships. "Let's look for a place here." And he set off, looking for a cheap B&B by the docks. It was at this moment, that Joan knew Bill was working as a driver behind her back, and then she was no longer silent.

∞

So Bill had to retire for real this time.

Joan didn't like the stage 3 tuned rally Saab that Bill drove, and suggested (demanded) that he got rid of it.

"Why don't you get a mini, like Jill. It doesn't need new tyres every three months like yours."

And so Bill was sent off to the auctions to sell his car and buy a replacement. He came back with a Humber sceptre, which was much larger than the car he had sold.

"Why did you get such a big car?" asked Joan.

"So the go kart could fit in."

"Go kart?"

Bill had bought a racing go kart.

That weekend, Bill took Joan for a picnic, and they stopped at a nearby disused aerodrome to have their sandwiches and tea.

"What's all that noise?" asked Joan.

"I have no idea. Let's go have a look."

As chance would have it, it was a local go kart racing club and they were practising.

"What a stroke of luck," said Bill, unloading his go kart. "Maybe they'll let me have a go."

And so, Bill took up go karting. He was the East Anglia area champion three years running at age 60.

As long as Bill wasn't driving on the roads, Joan didn't mind too much, but in the end, she made him give this up as well.

Bill would sometimes go to the stores and just run the till and talk with customers, or he would pop down to the factory to see how they were doing, but it wasn't enough.

Within 6 months of really retiring and nothing to do, Bill died.

22.   A HOLTOM DEATH

I was at my mother's funeral when I met a couple of distant relatives from the Holtom side.

"We're sorry we couldn't come to the last do. No disrespect, but we had a funeral the same day," said a cousin.

"That's OK. Anyone I know?"

"Your great uncle Douglas."

I had no idea who this was, so I just nodded noncommittally, and they all sniggered.

"What?"

"Well, they say that if it is your time, then there's nothing you can do, and there was nothing he could do" said another cousin.

"What on earth do you mean?"

"I'll tell you." And so they did.

Doug's story.

Doug was one of Bill's brothers and he had organised a sponsored parachute jump for charity. He was 85 years old.

The idea was for him and a group of 5 others to jump out of a plane over Southend, and try to land onto a cross marked out on the beach. The closer they got, the more money they made.

On this particular day, God decided that Doug was going to die. It was his time.

The plane set off and flew toward Southend. The intention was for the pilot to fly parallel to the beach and drop the parachutists out, singly, one on each pass. Doug had organised it, and he would go last.

As the plane approached Southend, God poked his head out of the clouds and aimed his finger.

The engine spluttered and stopped.

God smiled.

The pilot fiddled with some switches and the engine restarted.

"Phew," said Doug.

"Bugger," said God.

"I have engine problems and I'm going directly back to the airfield. I can fly over the drop zone, but you will all have to jump out at once, instead of separately," said the pilot.

The all agreed and prepared for the jump.

"Now." And they all jumped out, Doug bringing up the rear.

Again God pointed his finger, "pop," he said, and Doug's chute didn't open.

Doug plummeted to earth, but he was an experienced parachutist, and cut away the useless chute and then deployed his reserve, which opened, and he resumed floating back to earth.

"Phew," said Doug.

"Bugger," said God.

Unfortunately, the delay in opening the chute had taken Doug away from the beach landing zone, and he landed in the sea, 200 yards off Southend beach, and drowned.

"Gotcha," said God.

Some of you will go, "oh no," and feel guilty that one of your initial responses to this was to laugh.

Please do. He would have wanted it that way. It was a Holtom Death.

Doug turned up at the pearly gates and nobody was there.

He rang the doorbell, and St Peter poked his head around the gate.

"Name?"

"Douglas Holtom."

"Hmm. Sorry there was nobody to receive you. We were expecting you earlier."

Printed in Great Britain
by Amazon